管理会计学刊

JOURNAL OF MANAGEMENT ACCOUNTING STUDIES

地　址

北京市朝阳区惠新东街10号对外经济贸易大学宁远楼国际财务与会计研究中心《管理会计学刊》编辑部

（邮编:100029　　电话:010-64493525　　传真:010-64493412）

北京市海淀区成府路205号　北京大学出版社209室

（邮编:100871　　电话:010-62750037　　传真:010-62556201）

管理会计学刊

第 5 卷　第 1 期
（总第 6 期）

目　录

JOURNAL OF MANAGEMENT ACCOUNTING STUDIES

Vol. 5 No. 1

CONTENTS

管理会计学刊 *JOURNAL OF MANAGEMENT ACCOUNTING STUDIES*
第5卷 第1期 Vol. 5, No. 1

变化动荡的环境下数字产品的管理会计:一些探索性思考

Michael Bromwich*

摘　要　本文的写作目的是,研究已经或可能对管理会计产生影响的环境变化,分析目前实践中的管理会计工具通过对组织提供必要的信息以对组织的决策和内部控制产生的影响,探究管理会计在理论和实践领域的变革。本文重点研究数字经济和数字产品的动态变化在为社会带来新的机遇和挑战的同时,为管理会计师带来了哪些机遇和挑战。

关键词　数字经济,灵活性组织,收入管理,协同设计,联合资源,战略管理会计

一、引　　言

本文以2012年在中国厦门举办的亚太管理会计协会的主题演讲为基础。这次演讲基于《管理会计:回顾与展望》一书部分章节的内容,该书由英国特许会计师公会赞助出版,用于2009年纪念其成立90周年(Bhimani and Bromwich,2010)。本文的目的是分析已经或可能影响管理会计的环境变化;指出目前实践中的管理会计工具为决策与控制提供恰当信息的程度;探究在充满新的生产方式、服务方式和创收方式的环境下,管理会计需要在实践上和理论上做出哪些变革,以更好地履行其提供恰当信息的功能。由于缺乏实证证据,本文的探索必然只能是推理性的。数字经济和数字产品对全社会影响之深不言而喻,本文重点关注数字经济和数字产品的动态变化为管理会计师带来哪些具体

* 伦敦政治经济学院CIMA会计和财务管理名誉教授,E-mail: M. Bromwich@lse. ac. uk。感谢我的同事Alnoor Bhimani教授在这个领域多年来所做的努力。感谢戴天婧博士组织翻译此文。

的挑战和机遇，以及管理会计方法的变革。本文提出一些可行的管理会计新方法，旨在创建对管理会计变革讨论的良好氛围，鼓励研究者以解决问题为研究导向，提供更多实用的可选方案。

二、环境变化

对管理会计可能产生影响的社会环境变化包括：金融危机，全球化的加速发展，与日俱增的技术型流动组织，质量管理，数字经济的变革，更多的供销商合作关系和消费者合作关系的出现（包括消费者协同设计），组织结构的流动性增强（无边界组织），增多的管制，递增的风险和不确定性。这些变化多数依赖于电信行业的巨大变革，尤其是具有超高速宽带入口的光纤网络的广泛应用和智能手机的出现，以及计算机技术的革新，尤其是个人电脑和平板电脑的普及推动了全球化合作网络和全球化电脑网络的形成。

对于从事电视、报纸和其他数字媒体工作或与之相关工作的人来说，以上变化的特征已深入人心。这里，我们将重点介绍对管理会计有影响或可能产生影响的特征（详见 Bhimani and Bromwich，2009，2010，以获得更详细、更多的参考）。接下来，我们将讨论这些特征对管理会计的影响。

（一）全球化

众所周知，全球化指的是，社会存在空间和时间方面的彻底的根深蒂固的变化——削弱国家的空间或领土的重要性，加强国家之间在时间上和地域上的联系。根本地说，全球化就是指缩短国家之间和组织之间的虚拟距离。

乍看之下，全球化给组织带来的后续影响为管理会计师提供了很多机遇。在全球化组织中，管理会计师在会计核算方面发挥着重要作用：评估投资项目的价值和合资企业的价值，选择自制或外包决策。管理会计师还负责出具跨国活动的合并财务报告，根据不同组织单元和国家的文化差异制定和实施相宜的管理控制系统和绩效评估系统。通过会计信息的传递和管理控制系统的实施，管理层能够传达组织战略和计划到各个组织单元，有效减少地方影响。

毫无疑问，许多公司的会计师都成功地完成了这些任务。但是，在许多组织中，管理会计并未发挥其制定全球化战略的功能；通常为决策者，比如管理高层以及运营和业务发展经理，提供财务会计信息；对第三方提出的可选方案执行敏感性分析。有些战略决策属于“信仰行为”：为了引导竞争或跟上竞争，我们不得不进行财务分析。真正的战略评估和投资评估通常都由财务部门以外的、有制定战略决策需要的“影子部门”执行。

有些评论家认为，电信技术、信息技术、计算机网络和改善的组织网络推动了全球化进程。但是，管理会计师却不是这些功能的开发者，他们只扮演消费者的角色。

为了更好地适应以上变化，管理会计师应该培养战略眼光，加深对战略和技术相依性的理解，透过会计信息捕捉战略和技术之间的相关关系。

也有人认为，以上因素对管理会计并无影响，因此，管理会计师应该继续扮演好他们现有的角色，即成本记账员、信息提供者、投资的看门人和财务业绩评估者。这反映了少数全球化公司的现状，但是多数公司都已将战略导向彻底地贯彻到会计核算中。

（二）技术型流动组织

技术型流动组织，是指能够根据不同的产品需求和生产变型便利、迅速地调整生产流程的企业。大量新流程都与保障生产的灵活性有关。许多新流程都涵盖了所谓的灵活的组织技术。20 世纪八九十年代引进的许多新流程，如原材料需用量计划（MRP）、质量控制流程、企业资源规划（ERP）、适时采购和生产供应方法（JIT）、计算机辅助设计（CAD）以及计算机辅助生产（CAM）等，为这种灵活性的实现奠定了基础。流动性的进一步改善有赖于数字经济的发展、网络化的数字产品、新型供应网络和数字化的组织活动。

这些技术对传统的成本核算方法提出了挑战，它们会产生不同的成本核算结果，也会对资源耗费和资源流动状况做出不同的解释。数字产品的主要特征是，存在大量的前期资本投资和程序设计投资以及由此产生的高额固定成本，而固定成本的处理通常是传统管理会计的一大难题。

（三）购买方—供应商合作关系

购买方—供应商合作关系为越来越多的人所了解，它比以法律为基础的传统投标方法更灵活。供应商合作关系在交货时间、交货数量以及零部件的细节方面提供多种选择，也允许有经验的供应商确认质量。更广泛地说，这种合作关系为参与方之间互通有无提供了可能性和必要性，其沟通方式包括公开簿记的不同形式。供应商合作关系的工作依靠信任,而不是购买方事先制定的合法的、详细的说明书。更高级的合作关系允许供应商参与或受托完成购买方的设计活动(Hippel,2005)。在复杂的环境中,事无巨细的合约只会使合作关系所要求的灵活性受到限制。但是,这类合作关系要求组织和会计师分享从前被当作专有信息的资料(公开簿记)。有竞争力的供应商也会供应其他购买者,因此,供应商合作关系必须依赖购买者与供应商之间的共有知识和信息流。信任使一些现存的与投标供应合作关系有关的会计交易事项和质量控制成本不再被需要,同时淡化了管理会计师常用的控制指标的作用,比如价格、数量、退货数和质量波动。这是由于,经过一段时间后,供应商被信任能完成这些目标。供应商合作关系还要求双方客观披露各自的会计信息,接受合作方对本企业会计信息的分析,与合作方协商确定成本分配方法,从而使双方的会计系统都得到改善。

(四) 消费者合作关系

消费者合作关系、消费者设计或消费者协同设计可能不为人所知(Hallowell, 2002)。在数字经济的变革、互联网的兴起、数字产品的多样化之前,商家着力针对不同消费群体的需求提供各种特色的差异化产品。但是,消费者主要是“产品接受者”,市场提供什么产品就接受什么产品(所有的福特T型车都是黑色),除个性化产品外在产品设计上没有发言权。

互联网的兴起为消费者提供了更多的参与产品设计尤其是数字产品设计的机会,这样,消费者就从“产品接受者”变成“产品制造者”。为实现这一目标,电脑、移动手机和数字游戏通过在平台上供应大量的备选商品以便消费者各取所需。允许消费者自由选择加载内容的ipod便是一个典型的代表。社交网站极其依赖用户生成内容,网站用户可以通过应用程序获取目标消费产品。类似地,很多互联网平台都会提供推荐客户消费的软件。

互联网平台的“消费”实质是用户生成内容的消费,比如脸谱(Facebook)、维基百科(Wikipedia)。传统制造商也可以通过多种方式提高用户参与程度,比如,推广“产品设计游戏”,鼓励潜在消费者和现有消费者都参与其中。

消费者偏好导向促使新型产品与传统产品展开竞争:数字书凭借即时访问的个人图书馆代替了纸质书;在线供应商逐渐取代传统商店,比如书店。这种动态效应使很多早期科技变得冗余(如传真机),迫使传统制造商开发新产品或开发与消费者需求匹配的产品。如今，数字经济的冲击导致黑莓和诺基亚等早期移动手机产品领导者面临激烈竞争的市场环境。

对许多数字产品而言，价格与产量、消费量或用量之间的传统关系(收入是销量的线性函数)已不复存在。消费者在购买数字产品之初，为任何必要的硬件和软件支付一笔费用，实际消费时便不再发生支出，比如游戏。多数搜索引擎(如火狐浏览器)以及应用程序都供用户免费使用，支付率最高的应用程序通常购价低廉，并且使用免费。有些网站则提供免费的广告服务和网上购物服务。

因此，数字产品必须通过定价以外的方式收回成本，比如，收取广告费用、应用程序的网站发布费用、浏览器优先条目费用和版税。正如下面将要讨论的，这需要使用不同于传统模型的收益创造模型和成本回收模型，管理会计师需要为这类产品寻找成本动因。

(五) 无边界组织

合资企业广为人知，不管其运营重点关注的是国内市场还是国际市场。企业或企业的一部分缺乏特定的资源或者贷款时，会联合那些掌握这种资源或资金的企业组成临时企业或合作关系，这便构成了虚拟企业。当然，虚拟企业会面临与供应商合作关系同样的管理问题和管理会计问题——信息流的需求增强，公开账簿式会计接受客观分析，以及讨价还价问题。当代通信技术和持续的数字革命为不同所有制形式的企业之间开展广泛的沟通创造了必要条件和可能性。随着时间的推移，这些组织也许不再顾及个别公司的公司治理规范和管理控制系统，在一定程度上丧失了管理和沟通的独立身份和个体边界，从而凝聚成一个超越原有公司界限的超级组织(Merchant and Van der Stede，2007)。

虚拟公司的成员可能包括供应商、顾客，甚至竞争对手，他们通常是来自不同行业的广泛分布于世界各地的企业。这类企业的生存和运转依赖数字经济，其核心特征是流动性、灵活性和信任。合约是必要的，它规定了虚拟企业的建立原则。

企业通常要调节管理会计和会计工作中出现的紧张关系，甚至在外包企业和合资企业也如此，这些问题可能在无边界企业和虚拟企业中更为普遍、更为严重。所有制的建立、公司治理模式的构建以及参与各方文化的调节都不能一蹴而就。

由于虚拟企业的参与各方不可能制定完整的、涉及所有的未来重大不确定事件的合约，因此参与方承担了很大的风险，这也给企业的管理会计工作带来诸多不便。所以，这类企业的参与方容易被风险套牢。那些已经重金投资于企业的基础设施建设或作此打算的参与方都面临着这样的风险：未来谈判过程中，其他参与方会设法利用投资公司承担的沉没成本为自己谋利。这些因素都要求企业放松管制，加强合作（Straub，2004，300）。前文讨论的其他类型的新型组织也可能受这些结果的影响。

传统的管理控制系统实质上以资源投入为基础，重点通过正式的、集中的预算计划和控制最大限度地提高资源的利用效率。供应商合作关系、无边界企业和虚拟企业都在一定程度上属于产出控制导向，重点监控产出。这些企业还监测信息的及时性和信息质量。以上关于新组织形式的讨论表明，这些会计实体的管理会计可能不需要太关注日常会计报告，而是更多地参与重大决策的制定。可以说，这个领域的管理会计研究相对较少。

（六）管制

所有组织都面临着与日俱增的管制，这些管制既有长久以来就形成的，也有来自新增的受管制领域。其中包括一些完善的规定：税收征管，健康和安全法规（包括环境污染的防治和惩罚），职工福利，激励国内竞争和国际竞争以及设施管理。新近的规定包括：维护养老金，防止全球变暖，推行绿化经济，增强对金融市场和银行的监管，通过改善公司治理方法提高组织的透明性，要求不同类型的组织包括非营利组织规范财务报告的格式和其他报告的格式。这些领域中很多由超国家机构甚至是全球性机构监管，监管过程中自然困难重重，国际会计准则（IASB）便致力于将其监管范围扩展至全球。但是，许多领域的管制重点都放在国内，尤其涉及执法方面。

也许令人意外的是，会计研究与实践会计都没有阐述管制对企业成本的影响（Bromwich and Bhimani，1994，103—104）。但是，我们有理由认为，管制成本至少可以达到一般企业成本的20%，在一些管理体制下可能更高。对那些特定的监管者重点关注的企业和政治上可见的企业而言，这部分成本更高。众所周知，英国石油公司（BP）为在墨西哥湾造成的石油污染支付了巨大的成本。最近刊载在《经济学人》上的一篇文章预测，最新出台的针对英国银行业的准则可以使英国自2012年起五年内GDP下降0.7%，文章还引用了麦肯锡的一项研究结果，如果世界上最大的银行不采取措施抵消新准则的影响，它们在投资银行的净资产收益率将从2010年的20%左右下降到7%左右(Economist,2011)。

管制的第一个重要特征是，组织外部的管理者施加于组织的要求具有强制性。管制所要求的活动可能不是组织在无管制条件下会采取的最优行为。这些准则可以通过多种途径施行：如果组织不愿意遵守准则，最严重的后果是被关闭，其他与不遵守规则相关的惩罚措施包括刑事诉讼、经济惩罚或罚款。除了因落实准则要求和背离最优行为发生的成本外，组织至少还会承担另外两种管制所引起的成本。一是现存准则含义的不确定性，未来准则变化的不确定性，甚至管制机构变化的不确定性；二是企业为了规避成本昂贵或可能有损组织利益的准则而发生的活动重组成本。

就管理会计师目前的考虑而言，由于管制成本不直接受组织控制且其成本动因由组织外部机构确定，所以管制成本需要单独列示并定期报告。管理会计师需要通过理解这些成本动因，调查其变化过程，执行组织业绩对成本动因变化的敏感性分析，从而对可能的管制不确定因素有更好的理解。管理会计师若想规避准则，则需制订成本计划。

为了规避准则，有些组织只能终止某些活动或变换管制环境——金融机构似乎通常会做出这样的威胁。但是，如前文指出，对活动进行适当的调整来规避准则或减弱准则的影响也是可行的。比如，替换原材料，节省特殊生产程序；使用专用机器，降低工作的危险性；重组机构，应对关于反竞争的投诉。当然，管制不都是对组织有害的，比如绿色规则。管理会计师的责任就是分析管制对组织的不同作用。

这些领域都有待研究和实践的检验。

三、管理会计和数字产品

数字产品包括网页浏览器(如Internet Explorer、Netscape和百度)、搜索引擎(如谷歌、必应、雅虎和360安全浏览器)、游戏、应用程序、智能手机、平板电脑、移动媒体播放器、社交网站、在线购物服务、数字杂志和数字书，它们推动管理方法和会计方法的重要变革。接下来我们将简要介绍一些关于数字产品的管理会计问题。

首先，大多数字产品的收入和成本不遵循传统会计中的收入和成本模型。

传统会计认为，产品的单价不随产量的变化而变化（至少短期内成立），并且价格直接由消费者支付。类似地，在一定的资本资源范围内，单位变动成本不随产量的变化而变化。这里，变动成本是投入资源的价格和生产技术水平的函数。令投入资源的价格不变，则成本由企业的生产技术水平决定。传统的线性成本函数中要求每单位产出上的投入组合和数量不变。资本资源的成本和其他不能追溯到销量的成本都被看作固定成本。一些企业根据传统的成本模型假设，通过使用作业成本法为固定成本分配成本动因，让固定成本随成本动因的变化而变化(Bromwich and Hong，1999)。

（一）收入

管理会计师过去甚至现在都倾向于关注成本细节却忽略收入；由于组织中的其他部门通常掌握收入信息，所以大家都认为管理会计师不了解收入行为。这在传统模型下无可厚非，因为收入是销量和产品组合的线性函数。许多数字产品的消费是免费的，因此产品成本需要通过其他方式来补偿。一般来说，数字产品提供广义信息或娱乐服务。许多数字产品实际上是不同信息服务的捆绑销售组合。

众所周知，信息产品的收入不能像诸如汽车的传统产品那样简单地根据产量确定。信息产品的收入必然与信息消费量不直接相关。电视台的收入由三部分构成，即许可证收入、时间订阅表收入和广告收入。报纸主要依靠广告收入补偿成本。搜索引擎和免费应用程序的收入来源是广告收入。浏览器通过版税赚取收入。有些数字产品向消费者收取定额订阅费，但使用免费——比如图书馆购买的数字杂志。

信息产品与传统商品的差异性特征引发了定价问题。普通商品的特征是，商品在消费者的使用过程中被耗尽。普通商品被个人或组织购买后，便不能再为其他人所用。如果其他人也想消费这种商品，那么他们必须付费购买使用权。相反，信息产品不会在消费中耗尽，它们不能像传统商品那样在商店或百货大楼出售。信息具有低成本或零成本可获得性。因此，信息可以被称为联合资源——它可以被消费者联合使用，但是传统商品只能供个人使用。更专业地说，信息产品不具有消费竞争性，但是传统商品具有消费竞争性——只有一个人可以购买某件特定商品。财务报告包含的信息不因任何人的消费而贬值。整套财务报告的信息被一些人使用后，仍可以为其他人所用。数字杂志中的文章也不局限一个人使用。实际上，信息的广泛使用会产生网络效应，经很多人使用过后的信息产品反而会升值，比如社交网络和流行电视节目。

消费联合性或消费无竞争性是公共产品[1]的一大特征。公共产品能够被应用于多种活动，并且成本较低或不发生成本。数字产品至少在一定程度上具有消费联合性的特征。由于数字产品的定价没有考虑其低成本或零成本的可获得性，因此，数字产品的市场价格不能反映其联合消费性的特征。数字产品的大量前期投入通常成为沉没成本。在这种情况下，如果生产者遵循经典的经济学要求，按边际成本定价，则他们没办法补偿成本。因此，新的定价模型应运而生（Cowen，1992，111—126）。

不同的数字产品对这一问题的解决方法不同：浏览器向搜索引擎收取版税，比如，火狐公司超过80%的收入来源于谷歌公司缴纳的版税；搜索引擎的收入主要来源于广告，社交网络也是如此——脸谱公司超过90%的收入由广告收入构成；智能手机和平板电脑的收入来源于基于期间和功能的订阅服务。

网页产品的管理会计师面临的问题是，成本是消费量和产品组合的函数，但是收入与消费量不相关。广告商的目标是对产品感兴趣的消费者或者具有重复购买行为的消费者，因此，广告商偏好选择那些有能力吸引这部分消费群体的网页服务器。但是，搜索引擎和社交网站的公开声明表明，他们希望通过自己的广告和新产品来最大限度地吸引消费者，而不只是吸引广告商这个目标客户群。网站管理的问题是调和这两个目标之间的矛盾关系。管理会计师负责寻找恰当的价值动因，既能扩大网站消费者群体，又能吸引广告商投资。由于广告商按广告点击率付费，因此，以上两个目标之间的冲突被掩盖了。以点击率为基础计算的收入可能与消费量不相关，尤其是广告点击率的分布比例受消费者人数、消费者素质和消费偏好的持久性制约。

管理层面临的更重要的问题是，收入与产品、服务或其他成本对象的数量不直接相关。除了网页产品外，捆绑销售服务的电信产品也面临着同样的问题。捆绑销售虽然能够提供更宽泛的服务和更丰富的产品，但相应地，捆绑产品定价高，并且存在强制消费问题。这意味着，收入必须以某种方式分配到对

[1] 除联合性以外，纯粹的公共产品还包括以下特征：同时供应性，不完全的产能约束，供应商的非排他性，消费者非自愿排他性和非自由处置性。信息产品可能在某种程度上具备所有这些特征。供应商的非排他性是公共产品的第二个重要特征。具备这一特征的电子产品多种多样。搜索引擎有时开放供应范围，但是，以订阅为基础的服务机构通常把产品的供应范围限定在付费消费者（Mueller，2003）。

应的产品、服务和其他成本对象中。简单的消费量分配基础便不再适用。这个问题在面向教育机构供应的数字学术杂志中表现得最为突出，消费者的偏好并不能反映在价格中，因为特定论文的点击量、下载量和影响因子并不代表读者的偏好。

数字产品的供应商面临着两个分配难题：传统的固定成本分配问题，以及数字产品收入分配的新挑战。管理会计师能够利用其专业特长解决收入分配问题。专业的会计师将采用与成本分配观念相似的收入分配观念。产品的增量收益(收益流失)是指，企业在产品的生命周期内生产的所有产品的总收入减去不生产被分析产品时所获得的收入。

设产品总数是 N，包括产品 1 到 n，现有产品(产品 1)的增量收益(IR)等于企业不生产产品 1 而损失的收入。

$$IR_1 = R\left(\sum_0^n R_i\right) - R\left(\sum_0^n R_{n-I}\right).$$

其中，$R\left(\sum R_i\right)$ 等于组织的总收入，$R\left(\sum R_{n-I}\right)$ 等于总收入减去产品 1 的收入。这里的增量收入包括产品 1 的撤销生产对其他产品产生的收益效应。这些效应取决于其他产品是产品 1 的替代品还是补足物。但是，如果产品 1 单独生产，则其增量收入只测量产品 1 的收益效应。数字产品的收入不一定是消费量的函数，所以，在考察收入时，可变成本的等价物也无从获得。沉没收入指债务人发生的坏账部分。

(二) 成本

我们已经讨论过，至少有些数字产品的生产活动投入了大量的前期投资，前期投资成本不随产量的变化而变化，投资的设备供多种服务和产品联合使用。不同数字产品的前期成本的用途也不同：浏览器的前期投资用于购置能从网站获取、展示和搜索信息的软件；搜索引擎和捆绑期刊的前期投资用于建立运算法则、大型数据银行和服务器；电信供应商的前期投资用于搭建实体网络和数字网络。主营业务离不开网站产品和大型数据银行的组织，比如提供机票在线预订服务的航空公司和普通的提供网络购物服务的组织，都存在着投资成本难以追溯到具体的成本对象的问题。这类成本的核心特征是，资源不受产能限制，一些程序和活动对资源的使用不会损害另一些程序和活动的使用。换句话说，管理层对资源的使用具有非竞争性和非排他性。这些成本具有联合使用的特征。

（三）范围经济

这类产品配置具有优势(Panzer and Willig,1977,1981;Teece,1980)。这样的资源配置方式促进了范围经济的产生。在同样的技术条件下,联合生产多种特定产品或服务比在不同的工厂各自单独生产同样数量的产品和服务节省成本时,就产生了范围经济。企业最好同时生产需要用到联合资源的产品或提供使用联合资源的服务,以方便它们共用这种资源,而不是在单独生产的基础上为了使用资源而各自安排相应的活动。由于单独生产产品或提供服务时要各自为联合资源支付报酬,所以成本更高。范围经济广泛存在于数字产品的生产中,生产数字产品的软件、网络和数据银行可以被多种服务使用。数字经济外的生产领域也存在范围经济,比如,不同种类的存货共同使用公共设备;非高峰期生产启用最大产能,产生的增量成本、增量管理费用和增量财务费用较小。反对者认为,在不确定和动荡的环境中,实现生产的灵活性比追求范围经济更为重要。但在数字经济背景下这并不是问题,硬件资源根据需要调整起来相对容易。为了实现生产的灵活性,应做好预期研究与开发。

实证证据表明,范围经济并不普遍,主要存在于特定的行业。比如,医院通常关注范围经济,范围经济和规模经济的存在推动了大医院归并服务,小诊所停业整顿。《前沿经济学》(*Frontier Economics*,2012)在英国的医学部门的样本中证明了范围经济的存在。Banker et al.(1997)在银行业中找到了时间跨度较大的范围经济的存在。理论上,数字经济时代应不乏范围经济的存在,但是缺乏相关实证证据的支持。这并不难理解,因为范围经济和规模经济往往是这些行业战略的最重要组成部分,关于范围经济和规模经济的信息具有专属性特征。

（四）联合资源的会计处理

联合资源的成本对研究公共商品成本的经济学家并不陌生(Sharkey,1989)。但对联合资源成本的会计研究还不多见。实践中,这些资源的成本被当作固定成本处理,在组织的各部门之间进行分配。

联合资源引起的固定成本通常被叫作“公共固定成本”或者“联合固定成本”。这类资源的成本应作为消耗资源的组织单元的增量成本处理,问题是目前缺乏追溯到组织单元的实证成本分配方法。成本分配具有主观随意性和偏倚性，并可能引起部门经理之间的博弈和冲突。因此，传统的分配方法不再有现实可行性(Atkinson and Stiglitz，1980，482—518)。

补偿原始投资成本的可能途径多种多样，但均不能产生可靠的成本估计结果。组织倾向于通过公平的、对组织损害最小的方法补偿原始投资成本。这些方法相当复杂，信息含量大，需要信息和资源在组织内的大量传递。[2]

接下来，我们讨论几种可行的实践方法(Bromwich and Bhimani，1994，109—116)。较明显的方法是，组织向组织单元分配成本时，用同样服务的市场价格作为上限标准。这类似于组织愿意为获得这项服务而支付的价格(转移价格)高于市场价格，组织单元只能选择退出竞争。这种方法存在的问题是，取得的任意市场价格都包含归属供应商的边际利润，且不同的内在计算方法会引起不同的规模经济和范围经济。

无论如何，这种方法对我们讨论的组织都不适用，市场上很难找到合适的等价物来衡量复杂的网络和庞大的数据库的价值。这里，估计基础设施成本的唯一可行方法是，估算那些资源和技术配置相似的组织的收购价格。但是，这些估计价格必须根据组织的预计超额收益(超过投资成本的利润)进行调整，并调整企业因不同计算方法引起的差异。当然，只有组织单元被允许退出组织的供应链而从市场上获得资源的条件下，这些估计价格才有意义。但是，组织通常为了保护中心供应，而对组织单元在市场上购置资源的数量进行限制。

另外一种途径是，组织按组织单元在购置和使用资源前商定的自愿支付的价格来计算成本。理想的话，这一价格应该等于组织单元因使用这种资源比不用时多获得的增量收入。但是，资源的可获得性较好，组织的核心部门可以运用对各组织单元信息的掌握和自身的权力而向个别单位分配较多的成本，出于这些判断，组织单元的经理很可能会低报他们自愿支付的价格(Mueller，2003)。这种集中的分配过程必然会损害分权管理的效果。通过这种方式得到的内部转移价格会严重偏离最优定价，反映了组织内部的议价能力，组织单元之间的博弈和组织结构。为此，组织可以通过制定激励措施督促经理“讲真话”。但是，这种做法会涉及发放补贴和征税的问题，对组织单元来说并不

[2] 比如，拉姆齐价格是组织单元可以承受的最大价格，而不是以用量为基础计算的价格，拉姆齐价格的制定使得征税引起的组织单元的业绩扭曲效应最小化。通常价格上升会导致销量下降，拉姆齐价格作为单位可变成本的标杆，反映了部门对销量引起的价格变动的相对承受能力。所以，价格发生变动时，需求相对稳定的部门所能接受的价格较高。拉姆齐价格使部门能够按照利润最大化的原则行事(Baumol et al.，1988)。

实用。

还有一种对联合资源定价的方式是，从利润中心开始提高组织级别，向上到部门和团队，最后到公司级别，直到那个级别的部门被关闭，资源也不再使用。这个过程孤立了使用这种资源的各个组织部门，使他们不再想谁该为该资源付费。因为这类资源由各部门联合使用，所以不可能把资源的成本追溯到各个部门，任何形式的分配都会扭曲决策的制定。因此，要求这些部门能产生足够的收入以补偿可变成本和特定的固定成本，并一起产生余下的收入以补偿使用联合资源的成本。图 1 说明了这种方法。

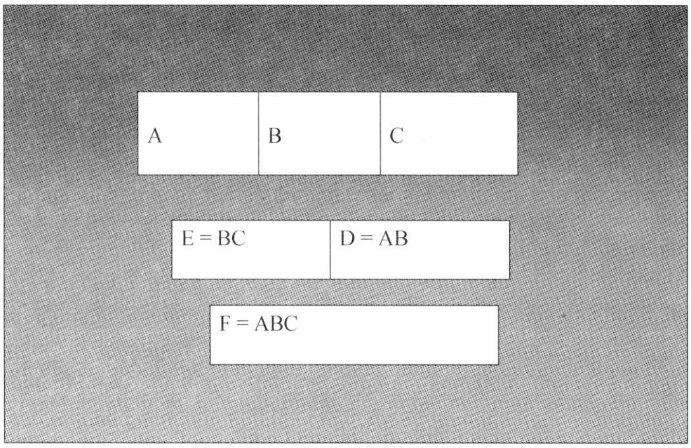

图 1　联合资源的分配

A、B、C 方格代表某销售数字产品企业的运营部门和销售部门 A、B、C 的可变成本和固定成本。每个组织单元分别负责营销一种数字信息服务，这些组织单元共用联合资源 D、E、F，D、E、F 方格分别代表对应资源的成本。B 部门和 C 部门共用资源 E，A 部门和 B 部门共用资源 D，三个部门联合使用资源 F。若 B 部门和 C 部门终止运营，则组织不再发生资源 E 的成本；若 A 部门和 B 部门中止运营，则组织不再发生资源 D 的成本。只有整个组织关闭，才不再发生资源 F 的成本，因此这是一项公司级别的费用。

组织要想成功运营，首先，每个运营和销售部门都需要单独产生足够的收入来补偿它们的可变成本和归属本部门的固定成本；其次，使用联合资源 D 和 E 的两个组合在补偿了本部门的直接成本后，还要产生足够的收入来补偿联合资源的费用；最后，在满足以上要求后，三个部门剩余的收入应该足够补偿资源 F 的成本。这种方法的好处在于，以上要求不至于使部门偏离经济最优行为，运营部门仍然可以遵循收入最大化原则。显然,如果组织不能满足这些要求,则需要重新考虑自己的战略。

表1用数据展示了以上模型。这里,我们假设A、B和C部门的可变成本分别是1000万元、2000万元和1200万元。资源D、E和F的成本分别是5000万元、5000万元和25000万元,包括主要数据库和必要的服务器的开发费用。这些成本的比例分配反映了数字产品企业的成本结构中联合成本的相对重要性。

表1 联合公共成本成本核算 单位:百万元

成本	A部门	B部门	C部门	AB总和	BC总和	ABC总和
可变成本	10	20	12			42
资源D的成本				50		50
资源E的成本					50	50
资源F的成本						250
总成本						392

按照收入最大化原则,A部门的收入应该满足以下要求:补偿本部门的变动成本,与B部门共同分担联合资源E的成本,在B部门和C部门补偿了各自的变动成本和联合资源D的成本后仍有剩余收入的前提下,与B部门和C部门共同分担资源F的成本。同理,对于B部门来说,其收入应该满足以下要求:补偿本部门的变动成本,与C部门共同分担资源D的成本,与A部门共同分担资源E的成本,在A部门和C部门有剩余收入的条件下,与这两个部门共同分担资源F的成本。英国最主要的电信企业BT通过在其监管账户(regulatory accounts)中使用以上成本计算方法,向监管机构展示了对使用其网络服务的经营者定价的合理性(BT plc.,2012,section 5)。

这种对组织的内部部门的定价方式确实有不足之处,其结果并不是通常所理解的"成本"。由于组织要通过实现决策时点的计划来收回投资,则组织对内部单元的定价不是成本,而应该是目标贡献。这种方式将引发讨价还价问题、博弈问题和部门冲突问题。个别部门认为,他们只需要支付属于自己部门的增量成本。也就是说,由表1知,A、B和C部门只需支付各自的变动成本。但是,管理层希望各个部门能共同分担联合资源的成本(Sharkey,1989,35—42)。组织单元的经理很难理解这种方法。

这种方法看起来比较抽象,但是,除了数字产品领域外,信息产品和智力资产的应用领域的联合固定成本也在增长。如何对联合资源进行会计核算,成为数字产品会计的重中之重。上文讨论过的方法是目前可行性最好的方法。这一领域对未来管理会计研究的重要性和挑战性不言而喻。

四、战略管理会计

动态和动荡的市场环境包含消费者市场和生产者市场的重大变化，战略管理会计（SMA）概念让注重实践的会计师看到希望（Simmonds，1981），也为生产数字产品的组织提供了管理会计的新思路。数字产品的生产企业需要在激烈的竞争环境中广泛地吸引消费者和广告商——我们只记得成功的产品，而大多数产品都失败了。这里，我们简要地分析一项调查。战略管理会计提供了旨在改善公司战略的多元化技术，要求会计师尽可能多地提供会计信息（Hoque，2006；Ward，1997；Bhimani and Bromwich，2010，48—52）。

目前，管理会计更重视组织内部，主要关注组织已发生的成本，寻求效率的改善，并制订短期计划。战略管理会计的支持者认为，消费者和竞争对手主要活跃于市场，因此会计应该提升对企业外部的市场的关注。战略管理会计属于管理会计的规范研究方法，不同的分析框架往往能得出一致的结论，并且能经得住实证证据的检验。

战略管理会计关注的问题主要包括：了解产品生命周期和战略生命周期内的成本，成本与价值驱动因素的关系，了解组织的成本结构和竞争对手的成本结构，确定实施战略的成本，与竞争对手实施战略的成本进行对比。管理会计师应关注与竞争者相关的价值增加，从长远上监控覆盖所有战略变量的市场业绩。

常用的战略管理会计工具包括：战略导向的作业成本法，目标成本法，竞争定位信息，竞争定价信息，竞争对手成本核算法，生命周期成本核算法，质量成本核算法，价值链成本核算法，产品属性的成本核算法（Guilding et al.，2000）。这些工具都与数字产品的供应商相关，但是企业应该重视产品属性的成本核算方法，重视比较产品属性成本与消费者愿意支付的价格，重视将这种方法扩展应用到广告商的价值动因的成本核算。

战略管理会计的主要研究方法是问卷调查法，调查管理层常用的战略管理会计工具是什么，哪些工具最具有未来价值。Guilding et al.（2000）是问卷调查法领域的主要文献，该文调查了新西兰、英国和美国的一些大型公司。新西兰和英国的问卷回复率较高，美国的问卷回复率较低。文章作者调查了12种战略管理会计工具，结果并不理想：战略成本核算法和基于消费者对产品属性评价的定价方法得分较高。基于价值的工具中，除了一项得分低，其他得分都较高。这表明组织对基于价值的工具的重视。最近的一份关于意大利最大的制造企业的调查问卷（Cinquini and Tenucci，2010）结果优化了Guilding et al.(2000)的调查结果，接受调查的大多数企业使用了多达10种工具。与此相反，对116家德国综合医院发放的调查问卷表明，这些工具都很少被用到（Lachmann et al.，2013）。这表明，我们有必要考虑不同的行业对战略管理会计用法的差异性，考虑不同行业文化及不同国家文化对战略管理会计使用的影响。

毋庸置疑，认为施行战略管理会计就是采用其所有工具的观点有一定的偏颇。实际上，战略管理会计的含义在实践中没有被充分理解。SMA的定义有很多种，包括针对战略管理会计工具的不同视角和不同侧重点。Langfield-Smith (2008)客观地解释了战略管理会计的定义，但其大部分证据都来源于有关作业成本法（ABC）的研究，其中只有一部分内容与战略角度相关。尽管如此，战略管理会计中依然有许多概念已被应用于实践，这表明战略管理会计在管理会计教学和咨询中发挥的重要作用。一些研究领域探究了那些能够反映动态和动荡的环境中存在问题的工具没有被使用的原因。有些人认为战略管理会计在数字产品行业被广泛使用，但这一观点还没有证据支持。

五、结　　论

我们认为，大多数环境变化都为管理会计师提供了挑战和机遇。在讨论环境的变化时，我们为管理会计师提出了如何应对这些变化的建议。这些建议在接受实证证据的检验之前都还只是推论。理论研究应该提出更多的可选方案，但是案例研究、实地研究和调查研究工作也亟须加强。

当考察数字产品时，会计师似乎要考虑很多调整传统的成本结构的问题。虽然传统会计把消费量作为成本动因，但是数字产品定价却不一定与消费量相关。更极端的情况是，消费量可能与生产成本的补偿完全不相关。搜索引擎的成本通过广告收入补偿，但消费者可以免费使用。广告商的需求与消费者的服务消费量只是间接相关。数字产品的收入模型必然与传统收入模型大不相同。由于数字产品的供销商提供了大量的服务，所以企业不仅需要把固定成本分配到产品，还要分配收入。简单的收入分配基础，如广告点击率数量，可能是主观的，不一定反映服务的价值动因。确定一种产品或服务的增量收入时要格外谨慎。

数字产品的主要问题是存在大量的前期投资，其特点表现为，投资的资源一旦投入使用，消费者便能够以很低的成本或零成本使用这种资源。因此，这类资源的成本与用量无关。我们回顾了很多处理这类资源成本的方法。这些资源的耗费都不产生成本，只是为用户活动确定价格，让这些资源的成本得以收回。已应用于实践的一种可行的分析方法是，联合使用特定资源的组织单元用补偿了本部门成本后的净收入分担联合资源的成本。这一领域有待继续分析和研究。

文章结尾提出了疑问：既然战略管理会计的技术能反映环境的变化，为什么企业没有对战略管理会计加以利用？

参考文献[3]

[3] 参考文献请见本文的英文版。

管理会计学刊
第 5 卷 第 1 期

JOURNAL OF MANAGEMENT ACCOUNTING STUDIES
Vol. 5, No. 1

Management Accounting in a Changing, Turbulent Environment with Digital Products: Some Exploratory Thoughts

Michael Bromwich *

Abstract The objectives of this article are to consider some of those environmental changes that either have or are likely to impact on management accounting, to indicate how far current management accounting tools used in practice can provide appropriate information for decision making and control in this setting and to speculate on some areas of change where management accounting either in practice or theory seems to need transformation. The focus will be on how the dynamics of the digital economy and new digital products which are of course raising new societal challenges and opportunities are similarly generating new challenges to and opportunities for management accountants.

Key words Digital Economy, Flexible Organisations, Revenue Management, Co-design, Product Jointness, SMA

1. Introduction

This article is based on a plenary talk given to the Asia-Pacific Management Accounting Association's Annual Conference in Xiamen China in 2012. This talk was itself based on parts of the book *Management Accounting: Ret-*

---

* CIMA Professor of Accounting and Financial Management Emeritus, London School of Economics and Political Science. E-mail: M. Bromwich@lse. ac. uk. My thanks are due to my co-worker in this area Professor Alnoor Bhimani for all his efforts over many years.

rospect and Prospect which was sponsored by the Chartered Institute of Management Accountants (CIMA) as part of the celebration of its 90th anniversary in 2009 (Bhimani and Bromwich, 2010). The objectives of the article are to consider some of those environmental changes that either have or are likely to impact on management accounting, to indicate how far current management accounting tools used in practice can provide appropriate information for decision making and control in this setting and speculate on some areas of change where management accounting either in practice or theory seems to need transformation in order to provide appropriate information in environment with new methods of production and of service provision and new methods of revenue generation. This exploration has to be perforce speculative because of the lack of empirical evidence. The focus will be on how the dynamics of the digital economy and new digital products which are of course raising new societal challenges and opportunities are similarly generating new challenges to and opportunities for management accountants that may require radical new approaches in management accounting. Possible approaches are suggested for some of the new challenges to generate a debate on possible changes to management accounting and to stimulate researchers to both generate other possibly more useful options and to focus their research on finding new solutions.

2. Environmental change

Changes in the environment impacting on society and likely to affect management accounting include financial crises, accelerating globalisation, increasing technologically "fluid" organizations, quality management, changes in the digital economy, more supplier and consumer partnerships including consumer involvement in product design, increasingly fluid organization structures (organizations without boundaries), increased regulation and either increased risks or different uncertainties. Most of these alterations depend very strongly on recent vast changes in the telecoms industry, especially extensive optic fibre networks enabling super-fast broadband access, advanced mobile (cell)phones and on similar changes in computer technology especially personal computers and tablets/slates allowing global networking and universal access to the worldwide web.

The characters of most of these changes are well known to most people from television, newspapers and other data sources and generally working with and through many of them. Here the less obvious ones are described briefly concentrating on those impacting on and likely to affect management accounting. (See Bhimani and Bromwich, 2009 and 2010, for more detail and additional references). Some of the management accounting implications of several of them will be discussed later. Some implications for others will be discussed briefly below.

2.1 Globalisation

As is well known the globalisation of activities refers to: sweeping and deep seated changes to the spatial and temporal aspects of social existence—diminishing the importance of national space or territories and compressing the temporal and locational relations between countries. Fundamentally it refers to diminishing the virtual distance between countries and between organisations.

At first sight the consequent changes in organisations due to globalisation raise a lot of opportunities for management accountants. They seem to have strong role in accounting for global organisations where they are often involved in the appraisal of investments and of joint ventures and make or buy decisions and outsourcing. They are also responsible for the reporting of the consolidated financial results of internationally widely spread activities and devising and applying management control systems and performance measurement systems in diverse locations with different cultures both within organisations and nationally. Accounting information and management control systems are often the major method by which organisational strategies, and plans are conveyed to organisational elements and which act to reduce local influences.

There is no doubt that in many companies accountants have been very successful in these tasks. However in many organisations management accounting does not play a substantial role in determining global strategy; often providing only financial accounting information to the decision makers, such as senior management, operation functions and business development executives, and appraising and conducting sensitivity analysis on options suggested by others. At least some strategic decisions are "acts of faith" of the type: we must do it to lead or to keep up with the competition which do not lend themselves to financial analysis. Often the real appraisal of strategies and investments are undertaken by "shadow departments" outside finance who are seen as more sympathetic to the needs of strategic decisions.

Some commentators believe that advances in telecoms, IT, the Internet and improved organisational networks have enabled globalisation. Generally, management accountants do not "own" any of these functions in organisations and often play only a consumer role in these areas.

With this view it can be argued that management accountants need to respond to the above factors and become much more strategic understand that strategy and technology are intertwined and that management accounting needs to capture strategic and technology interdependencies in the information they provide.

The alternative view is that, most of the above factors associated with globalisation do not impinge on management accounting and therefore management accountants can continue to play their existing roles as cost bookkeepers, information providers, investment gate keepers and financial performance measurers. There is some evidence that this is what is happening in some global firms but others full heartedly adopt a strategic orientation in accounting.

2.2 Technological "fluid" organizations

This refers to firms that have organised their production processes so that these processes can easily and quickly be adjusted to demands for different products and production variants. A very large number of new processes are relevant to assuring production flexibility. Many new processes comprise what has been called flexible organisational technology. The foundations for this flexibility were laid by the introduction in 1980s and 1990s of a number of processes including material requirement planning (MRP), quality control processes, enterprise resource planning (ERP), just in time purchasing and production supply approaches (JIT), computer aided design (CAD) and manufacturing (CAM). Further fluidity required the development of the digital economy and its new networking opportunities with new digital products, new supply networks and the digitalisation of organisational activities.

Many of these techniques challenge conventional costing results, first by generating alternative figures and secondly by providing different pictures of resource consumption and flows. Major characteristics of these developments are that they require very large upfront capital investment and investments in major planning processes generating high fixed cost investments which as is well known are often not well handled by conventional management accounting.

2.3 Purchaser-supplier partnerships

Purchaser-supplier partnerships are becoming better known and are much more flexible than the conventional legal based tendering approach. Supplier partnerships allow options on the timing and quantities of delivery and parts and on component specifications and with experience allow quality to be vouched for by the suppliers. More generally these partnerships allow and require much more communication between the parties including variants of open book accounting. They work by substituting trust for reliance on up-front purchaser's legal and detailed specifications. More advanced partnerships allow the supplier to either participate in or have delegated to them some of the purchaser's design activities (Hippel, 2005). The great flexibility required by these partnerships is likely to be constrained by any attempts to write detailed contracts in a complex environment. Such partnerships do however require organisations and their accountants to share what has been regarded as proprietary information (open book accounting). They have to rely on mutual knowledge and information flows between the purchaser and competitive suppliers who may also supply other purchasers. Thus trust is necessary but this allows much of the existing transactional accounting and the quality control costs associated with tender based supply relationships to be given up allowing the abandonment of some of the management accountant's favourite controls, such as price, quantity, returns and quality variances. This is because over a period of time suppliers are trusted to meet such targets. However partnerships also open both parties' accounting systems to critical exposure, analysis and bargaining over allocation methods leading to mutually worthwhile improvements.

2.4 Consumer partnerships

Consumer partnerships and consumer involvement in design and even co-design are, perhaps, less well known (Hallowell, 2002). Prior to changes in the digital economy, the rise of the internet and the availability of a great variety of electronic products, efforts were made to provide differentiated products with a variety of characteristics that appealed to different groups of consumers but consumers were mainly product takers where consumers have to take what is offered on the market (all model T Ford cars were black) and have no say in product design except for personally tailored products.

The internet especially has given greater opportunity for consumer involvement in product design especially with digital products. Here, the consumer becomes a product maker rather than a product taker. Computers, mobile phones and electronic games achieve this by providing a large number of options on a platform from which the consumers can chose those of utility to them. An outstanding example of this is the iPod where the loaded content is chosen by the consumer. Social websites rely substantially on customer generated content and the users of the websites can chose much of the content they wish to consume via APPs. Similarly, consumption on many internet platforms requires the use of consumer introduced software.

With many platforms "consumption" is the consumption of customer generated content, for example, with Facebook. com and Wikipedia. com. More conventional manufacturers can also involve the consumer in a variety of ways, for example by promoting "product design games" that involve potential and actual consumers.

The dynamics of incorporating consumer preferences has led to new products competing with conventional offerings: e-books substituting for books with instantly accessible personal libraries. Online suppliers are ousting conventional shops and stores, bookshops for example. The effect of this dynamic has rendered many of the earlier innovations either redundant (for example FAX machines) or subject to great challenges to provide new or matching opportunities to consumers. Such attacks have generated the currently severely contestable markets now facing the earlier mobile phone product leaders-the Blackberry and Nokia organisations.

For many digital consumer products the conventional relation between price and units of production/consumption /usage where revenue is a linear function of sales is severed. With many digital products the consumer pays an amount for any necessary hardware and software but then pays nothing for actual usage, games for example. The use of many search engines, such as Firefox is free as are many APPs and most paid-for Apps are cheap to purchase and usage is free. Many websites are provided free as either a means of advertising or as part of on-line purchasing.

The costs of digital products therefore have to be paid by means other than pricing per unit, such as fees for advertising, publishing Apps on websites and prioritising browser entries and royalties. As will be discussed below this may require the use of different models to the traditional ones for revenue generation and cost recovery and different revenue and cost drivers will need to be used by management accountants for these types of products.

2.5 Organisations without external boundaries

Joint ventures with either a national or international focus are well known. Virtual firms or enterprises are comprised of independent firms or parts of firms that form temporary partnerships or enterprises with those who have the specific resources required to achieve a given goal beyond the ability of the individual enterprise making up the virtual enterprise and allow access to funding not otherwise available. These of course face some of the same management and management accounting problems as suggested above to be encountered by supply partnerships—the need for major information flows, open book accounting with critical analysis and bargaining. Contemporary communications technology together with the continuing digital revolution have enabled and made necessary extensive communications amongst firms in any sort of partnership. Over time, perhaps, irrespective of formal corporate governance requirements and the formal management control systems of the individual companies, these organisations in their management and in their communications lose a degree of their separate identities and their individual boundaries and may agglomerate into a super organisation which no longer respects the boundaries of the original firms (Merchant and Van der Stede, 2007).

The members of the virtual enterprise may be suppliers, customers and even rivals and encompass firms from very different industries, often widely dispersed across the world. Such enterprises rely on the digital economy to exist and to operate. Essential characteristics are fluidity, flexibility and trust. Contracts are necessary but now lay down only the principles upon which the virtual organisation is founded.

In terms of management accounting and accounting generally there are a number of tensions that have to be reconciled even in outsourcing and joint ventures and these are likely to be more numerous and severe with enterprises without boundaries and virtual enterprises. The structuring of ownership may be very difficult as may the required pattern of corporate governance and reconciliation of the parties' different cultures.

One reason for these difficulties is that the parties in the virtual enterprise bear a number of risks arising from these endeavours as it is impossible to determine complete contracts covering all future major contingencies. All the parties in these types of enterprises may therefore be, for example, subject to "hold up" risks. Any party that has made or makes investments that are substantially of value only in the enterprise faces the risk that in later bargaining the other parties will seek to take advantage of the sunk cost borne by the investor firm. These factors may mean looser controls and more emphasis on achieving co-ordination (Straub, 2004, 300). These influences may also affect the other new organisational forms discussed above.

Conventional management control systems are substantially input based. The concern is to maximise the efficiency of the use of resources via formal and centralised budgetary planning and control. Supplier partnerships, firms without boundaries and virtual enterprises all to a degree are more orientated towards output controls so as to monitor outcomes. They will also monitor the timeliness and quality of information. Our discussion above of all the new forms of organisation suggest that in such entities management accounting may need to be less concerned with routine accounting reports and more involved with aiding major decisions as they arise. It is fair to say management accounting research in this area is relatively sparse.

2.6 Regulation

All organisations are facing increased regulation both of long established types and in many new regulated areas. These include well established requirements: the collection of taxes, health and safety legislation including avoiding and penalising environmental pollution, workers' welfare, encouraging competition, both locally and internationally, and the control of utilities; more recent concerns include: protecting pensions, avoiding global warming and facilitating the "greening" of the economy, new requirements on financial markets and banks, improving the transparency of organisations via corporate governance approaches and the required forms of published financial and other reports from many different types of organisations including non-profit organisations. Many of these areas are regulated by super national organisations or even globally with all the difficulties that these entail—the scope of the International Accounting Standards Board (IASB) is aimed towards being global. However, many of the areas of regulation have an intentionally strongly national focus especially with regard to enforcement.

Perhaps surprisingly, the effects of regulation on firms' costs have not figured substantially either in the research or practical accounting literatures (Bromwich and Bhimani, 1994, 103—104). However it seems not unreasonable to suggest that these costs could amount to at least 20 percent of the costs of average firms and higher in some regimes. These costs could be much higher for firms that are the focus of specific regulators and are politically visible. The enormous costs to BP of oil pollution in the Mexican Gulf are well known. In a recent article the *Economist* estimated that the recent new rules on UK banks could depress gross domestic product GDP in the UK by 0. 7 percent over the 5 years from 2012 and quoted a McKinsey study that said if the world 's biggest banks did nothing to offset the impact of the new rules, their returns on equity in investment banking would fall from about 20% in 2010 to about 7% (Economist, 2011).

The first important characteristic of regulation is that some authority outside the organisation imposes actions on the organisation. The activities required may not be what the organisation would otherwise regard as optimal behaviour. These prescriptions can be enforced in a number of ways. With the most severe the organisation can be closed down if it is not willing to follow the regulations, other failures to adhere to the regulations can mean criminal prosecutions. Other breaches may incur financial penalties or fines. Apart from the cost of implementing regulatory requirements and having to deviate from otherwise optimal behaviour, organisations experience at least two other costs imposed by regulation. The first is regulatory uncertainty both in terms of what extant regulations mean and the possibility of different regulations in future or even facing a different regulator later and the second is the cost of rearranging activities to avoid regulations which are seen to be expensive or likely to damage the organisation.

As far as the management accountant is concerned regulatory costs need to be shown separately from other costs and reported frequently as these costs are not directly under the control of the organisation and their drivers are determined outside the organisation. The management accountant needs to understand these drivers, investigate how they may change and determine the sensitivity of the organisation's performance to alterations in them thereby aiding in understanding possible regulatory uncertainty. The management accountant would need to cost plans to avoid regulations.

Some regulations can only be avoided by ceasing an activity or moving it to a different regulatory regime—a threat that financial organisations often seem to make. However, as was suggested above it may be possible for organisations to legitimately alter their activities to avoid regulations or reduce their impact. For example an alternative material can be substituted for one that that requires special procedures in its use. Dangerous jobs can be avoided by using special machinery. Complaints concerning anti-competitive behaviour may be met by restructuring the organisation. Of course not all regulations are suboptimal for organisations. This often is argued in favour of "green" regulations. The management accountant's role is to provide analysis for these types of decisions.

All these areas would seem to provide opportunities for research that could also aid practice.

3. Management accounting and digital products

Digital products include web browsers like Internet Explorer, Netscape and Baidu, search engines games such as Google, Bing, Yahoo and 360 Secured Browser, games, Apps, smart phones, tablets and slates, mobile media players, social websites, on-line shopping and electronic journals and books. They require major changes in management methods and in accounting approaches. Here we will briefly look at some of the management accounting problems.

The fundamental problem is that most digital products do not follow the conventional pattern assumed for product revenues and costs in accounting. The traditional model assumes that revenue is the same per unit of product (at least in the short run) irrespective of volume and this price is paid directly by the consumer. Similarly variable cost is assumed to be the same per unit irrespective of volume subject to the amount of capital resources provided. Here variable costs are a function of input prices and technology. If we hold input prices constant then cost behaviour is generated by the technology used. A linear technology that uses a constant mix and quantity of inputs for each unit of output is required to generate the traditional linear cost function. The cost of capital resources and other resources that cannot be traced to sales volume are treated as fixed costs. Activity based costing (ABC) is used by some firms in order to convert some fixed costs into costs variable with cost driver volumes but shares the same assumptions as the traditional model (Bromwich and Hong, 1999).

3.1 Revenues

In the past, and perhaps even now, management accountants have tended to focus on costs often in great detail and tended to neglect revenues and usually were (and, perhaps, now are) regarded as not really understanding revenue behaviour—others in the organisation often "own" revenue information. With the traditional model this may be reasonable where revenue is a linear function of volume and product mix. With many digital products there is no charge for consumption therefore the cost of products needs to be recouped in other ways. Generally digital products provide information widely defined or entertainment. Many digital products are really bundles of different information services.

It is well known that payment for information cannot be easily based directly on product volumes as is the case with conventional products, such as motor vehicles. Rather the charges for information based products have to be, perforce, be more indirectly related to the consumption of information. The funding of television programmes is thus usually via either purchasing a licence or a time based subscription to watch or by payments from advertisers. Similarly newspapers are mainly paid for by advertising revenue. Search engines are often paid for by advertising among other sources as are many free APPs and browsers by royalties. Other products levy fixed charge subscriptions on consumers but usage is free-bundles of electronic journals sold to libraries provide an example.

This pricing problem arises because information has different characteristics than conventional goods. Such goods are "used up" by purchase. If a unit of a usual good is purchased by an individual or organisation, it is rendered unavailable to others. If others want to consume a unit of the good they must purchase a unit of their own. In contrast information-type products are not used up in consumption and therefore unlike conventional products information cannot be easily sold in shops or departmental stores. Information has the characteristic that once provided it can be made freely available to others at little or no cost. Thus it can be called a joint resource—it is available for joint use by consumers whereas conventional goods are single use. More technically, consumption of information can be characterised as non-competitive in use or consumption whereas that of a specific unit of a conventional goods does involve competition in consumption—only one person can purchase a specific unit. The information in financial reports does not depreciate with consumption by any individual. After use by somebody the complete set of information is still available for the use by others. Similarly the use of article from an electronic journal does not foreclose its use by others. Indeed greater use often produces network effects where a product is appreciated more when used by a greater number of people as seems to be the case with social networking sites and popular television programmes.

Jointness or non-competitive consumption is one property possessed by what are called public goods.[1] They are able to be used for a number of activities without cost or with a small cost. Digital products possess to at least a degree this attribute which may be called jointness in consumption. It is well known that this property will not be necessarily be fully captured by market prices because they will not "price in" the opportunity to provide others at little or no cost. Products of this type have a large up-front cost which is usually

---

[1] A pure public good possesses other attributes than jointness which include: simultaneous supply, non-exhaustive up to capacity constraint, non-exclusion by the supplier and non-voluntary exclusion by the consumer and non-free disposal. Information products may possess to a degree any of these characteristics. Non-exclusion by the provider is a second essential attribute of public goods. Digital products vary in their possession of this property. Search engines have this ability but use it sparingly whereas subscription based services are provided to only paying customers (Mueller, 2003).

"sunk". If producers in this situation were constrained to price at marginal cost, the classical economic requirement, they could not recoup their expenditure. Therefore other methods of pricing these goods have arisen (Cowen, 1992, 111—126).

Different digital products have solved this problem in different ways. The chosen methods include: for browsers royalties from search engines, thus Firefox gets over 80 percent of its revenue in this way from Google; for search engines revenue accrues mainly advertising as it does for social websites—it makes up over 90 percent of Facebook's revenue and for smart phones and tablets it is a duration and function based subscription.

A problem for management accountants for wed-based products is that costs are primarily a function of consumption volumes and product mix but revenue reflects such consumption perhaps only weakly. Advertisers seek those types of consumers that are likely to want to buy their products and are likely to repeat purchases. They will therefore favour providers that can show that they are able to attract such customers whereas search engine and social website organisations in their public statements seem to wish to maximise the number of users (consumers) by their own advertising and by offering new products. The problem for the management of websites is to reconcile the tension between these two objectives. Management accountants need to be involved by seeking the value drivers for both extra consumption and for attracting advertisers. This tension between generating consumption and advertising may be hidden where the advertisers are charged on the simple bases of, say, the number hits on their advertisements. Such charging bases are unlikely to generate revenue that is fully correlated with consumption especially where the mix of hits on advertisements changes with the number and quality of consumers and their pertinacity of preference for specific advertisements.

Perhaps a more important problem for management is that revenue is not directly related to products or services and other cost objects. This not just a problem for web based products but also applies to telecoms products where a number of services are bundled together. Bundles which provide greater volume of services and additional products are higher priced but they are still a bundle. This means that revenue has to be assigned to products, services and other cost objects in some way. It is unlikely that simple allocation measures will make economic sense in this situation. This problem is, perhaps, most extreme with bundles of academic journals supplied to educational organisations where hits, downloads and impact factors do not necessarily measure the value of "consumption" of an article to the consumer whose preferences are not necessarily reflected in prices.

Supplier organisations face two allocation problems; one is the usual one of allocating fixed overheads and the new one with many digital products is that of allocating revenue. Management accountants may be able to help with the latter problem with their skills in this area. Skilled accountants will try to use revenue concepts similar to those used with costs. Here incremental revenue (revenue lost) from a product refers to: the total revenues received by the organisation from all its products including the product being analysed over its product life less the revenues generated by the organisation's total revenue excluding the revenues received from the product being analysed.

The incremental revenue (IR) of an existing product (product 1) to the organisation equals the revenue lost if the product 1 were not produced where the total number of products is N comprised of products 1 to n:

$$IR_1 = R(\sum_0^n R_i) - R(\sum_0^n R_{n-1}).$$

where $R(\sum R_i)$ is the total revenue of the organisation and $R(\sum R_{n-1})$ is the total revenue of the organisation excluding product 1. However incremental revenue here would include any effects on the revenues of other products with the withdrawal of product 1. These effects depend on whether any of the other products are substitutes or complements of product 1. The standalone revenue of product 1 where it is assumed that that the product is produced separately would measure only the revenue flowing from the product. Above it was said that revenue was not necessarily a simple function of consumption with digital products so there is no direct equivalent of variable cost when looking at revenue. "Sunk" revenues would seem to refer to the bad debt element of debtors.

3.2 Costs

It has already been said that many of the activities used in the production of at least some digital products involve large up-front investment whose costs do not vary with production volume and generate inputs that are available to be shared between several services and products. The purposes of these large up front expenditures vary between digital products: for browsers it is the software that allows retrieval, display and navigation of information from the web, for search engines and bundled journals it is search algorithms, vast data banks and servers and for telecoms suppliers it is their networks, both physical and electronic. This problem of large scale investments whose costs cannot be traced to cost objects also applies to many organisations that rely heavily on websites and large data banks in their businesses, such as with on-line booking for airlines and on-line shopping in general. The essence of this type of cost is that they are generated by resources which when in place can be used by a variety of processes and activities without sacrificing their use by other processes and activities up to some capacity constraint. That is, use by managers within the organisation does not involve rivalry and it makes no economic sense to exclude potential users within the organisation. These costs have elements of jointness in use by the organisation.

3.3 Economies of scope

Of course there are advantages in these types of production configurations (Panzer and Willig, 1977, 1981; Teece, 1980). They basically give rise to economies of scope. These economies arise where it is cheaper to produce a given bundle of products or services together rather than producing the same volume of each of the products or services in separate standalone plants using the same technology as to produce the bundle of products or services. With joint resources it is better to produce products or services together where they can share such resources rather than on a standalone basis separately making their own arrangements for the services provided by the joint resource. The latter arrangements will more expensive as each product or service will have to pay separately for the joint resource. These economies are present in the production of many digital products with software, networks and data banks that can be used by many services. Perhaps more familiar examples outside the digital economy are the sharing of inventories between products, in utilities the use of capacity required to meet peak demand to satisfy for off-peak requirements for only a small incremental cost and corporate advertising and financing. Against this, it can be argued that searching for economies of scope may be less important than ensuring production flexibility in an uncertain and dynamic environment. However, the underlying hardware resources in the digital economy are relatively easy to alter to meet demand. Flexibility in production suggests why anticipatory research and development is so important in this economy.

The general empirical evidence is that economies of scope are found fairly infrequently and then mainly in certain industries. For example the presence of economies of scope is a crucial concern in hospitals where their presence together with that of economies of scale enhances the argument for consolidating services in larger hospitals and closing smaller hospitals. See, Frontier Economics (2012) who find evidence for some economies of scope in UK in a sample of hospital specialities. Banker et al. (1997) find evidence of scope economies in banking over a substantial time period. The theory discussed above suggests their presence should be substantial in digital industries but there is as yet little evidence on these industries. This not surprising as such economies seem as likely to be central to their strategies and information on economies of scope is therefore likely to be regarded as proprietary.

3.4 Accounting for joint resources

The problem of "costing" resources with jointness characteristics has long been recognised by economists in their concern to finance public goods (Sharkey, 1989). Accounting research in this area has been rather sparse. In practice the costs of these resources are just regarded as overheads and allocated across the organisation.

The type of fixed cost generated by such resources is sometime referred to as either a "common fixed cost" or a "joint fixed cost". The problem with these costs is that they can only be treated as incremental to that group of organisational units that use the resources. However, there is no empirically based method of tracing these costs to use by any of the group of organisational units using the resource. Allocating them is arbitrary, biased and likely to lead to gaming and conflict between managers. They are therefore impossible to cost with conventional methods (Atkinson and Stiglitz, 1980, 482—518).

There are a variety of possible approaches but they do not generate cost estimates. Rather they are intended to allow the recouping of the original investment cost by charging products or parts of the organisation in a way that is believed to equitable and least damaging to organisational profitability. Some of these approaches are very complex, very information intensive and require substantial information and resource transfers within the organisation. [2]

Here we will consider a few approaches that might be used in practice (Bromwich and Bhimani, 1994, 109—116). The obvious approach is to consider what the services provided by these resources would cost to buy on the market and use these prices as proxies for the maximum charges for the services in mind within the organisation. These prices would be maximums as if organisational charges (transfer prices) exceed market prices then units of the organisation would seek to opt out. There are general problems with this approach. Any prices obtained would include profit margins for the supplier and may use different technologies and these differing technologies may give rise to differ-

[2] For example using what are called Ramsey prices tries to minimise the performance-distorting effect of levying a tax on organisational units by levying a non-usage based charge founded on the amount of charge the units can bear. The charge is levied as a mark-up on unit variable costs which reflects the unit's relative ability to bear price changes measured in terms of the likely fall in sales with respect to price increases. So units with relative constancy of demand in the face of price changes bear the highest amount of the charge. Such charges minimise the distortion from profit maximising conduct and thus require the minimum deviation from this conduct (Baumol et al., 1988).

ent economies of scale and scope.

In any case this approach is probably irrelevant to the organisations we are considering as the equivalent to their very complicated websites and enormous data banks are unlikely to available on the markets. It may be that the only way to obtain a price for some of the large amounts resources comprising elements of the organisation's infrastructure would be to estimate the cost of taking over organisations having at least some resources similar to those used in the organisation and compatible with the organisation's technology. However such estimated prices would have to be adjusted (reduced) for estimates of any abnormal profits (profits over and above the cost of capital) they are expected to earn and adjusted for any differences in technology. Even if such prices were available they would only have bite if units of the organisation were allowed to opt out of organisational supply and use markets where available. Generally organisations do not allow substantial amounts to be purchased on the market by organisational units in order to protect central supply.

Another approach would be to charge organisational units what they say they would be willing pay to use the resources prior to the decision to acquire or construct the resource. Ideally this charge should be the incremental unit profit that would be generated by the organisational unit using the resource over that obtained when not using the resource. However, organisational unit managers may have incentives to understate their willingness to pay especially if they believe either that the resource will be made available anyway or that others will be willing to or be forced to pay for the resource if the centre of the organisation has enough information about organisational units and sufficient power to enforce the charges it has decided upon (Mueller, 2003). This centralised procedure may be inimical to decentralised management. The resulting transfer prices may be substantially removed from ideal economic charges reflecting inter-organisational bargaining and gaming and organisational structure. It is possible to give managers in this setting "truth telling" incentives. However this involves possible patterns of subsidies and taxes on units which are perhaps too baroque for practical use.

Another approach for a given jointly used resource is to move up the organisational hierarchy starting with profit centres and moving up to divisions and groups and finally moving up the corporate level until the point is reached where if the units at that level were closed the resource would no longer be needed. This procedure isolates the group of organisational units that use the resource in mind who should pay the resource's cost. Given that such resources are joint between the users, it is impossible to trace the resource's cost to the individual units comprising of the group sharing a given resource and any sort of allocation will distort decision making. What is therefore required is that each unit sharing in the use of a resource should generate sufficient revenue to cover its variable costs and specific overheads and *together* with other units sharing the resources generate remaining revenues to at least cover the cost of the shared resource. This approach is illustrated in Diagram 1.

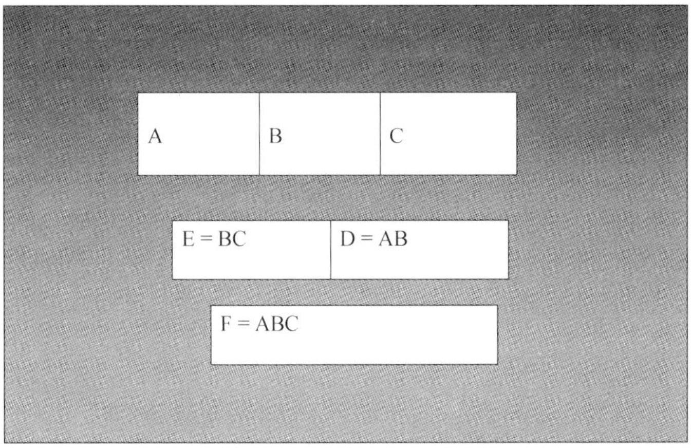

Diagram 1 Sharing the Costs of Joint Resources by Ascending the Organisational Hierarchy

Boxes A, B, and C represent the variable costs and any specific overheads of three operating and selling units, A, B and C of an organisation marketing digital products. Each unit markets one digital information service and each uses a number of joint resources from the set of resources D, E and F, the costs of which are shown in boxes E, D and F. Units B and C use resource E and units A and B use resource D and all three utilise resource F. The costs of resource E will only be avoidable if units B and C are shut down and the costs of resource D can be escaped only if units A and B cease operating. Closure of the whole organisation is the only way to cease incurring the cost of resource F. It is thus a corporate level expense.

For the organisation to succeed first each individual operating and selling unit needs generate enough revenue to cover its variable cost plus any specific overheads attributable to the unit and second the combined revenues of each of the two pairs of the two units using the joint resources D and E after meeting their direct cost must cover the costs of these two joint resources. Finally after meeting these requirements the remaining revenue from the three operating and selling units must be enough to pay for resource F. The attraction of this approach is that the operating units can still follow profit maximising behaviour without the above requirements distorting their optimal behaviour. Clearly if these requirements are not met the organisation needs to reconsider its strategy.

A numerical example based on the setting above is shown in Table 1. Here we assume that the variable costs of units A, B and C are 10 million, 20 million and 12 million respectively. The cost of resource D is 50 million, that for resource E is also 50 million and that for resource F is 250 million which includes developing major data bases and the necessary servers. The proportions of these costs are chosen to highlight the relative importance of joint common costs in the cost structure of, at least some, organisations selling digital products.

Table 1 Example of "Costing" Joint Common Costs

Costs(millions):	Unit A	Unit B	Unit C	$Total_{AB}$	$Total_{BC}$	$Total_{ABC}$
Variable costs	10	20	12			42
Cost of Resource D				50		50
Cost of Resource E					50	50
Cost of Resource F						250
Total						392

With this approach unit A following profit maximising behaviour would be expected to earn sufficient revenue to cover its variable costs and in combination with unit B to cover the cost of the joint resource E and to have sufficient remaining revenue so that together with the remaining revenues of the other two units after they have met their variable and joint cost they incur together to pay for resource F. Unit B after covering its variable cost would need to generate sufficient revenue to cover the costs of joint resources D and E in cooperation with units C and A respectively and have sufficient additional revenue to meet the cost of resource F together with the remaining revenues of the other two divisions. BT the UK's major telecoms organisation uses this approach in its regulatory accounts to justify to the regulator the prices it charges to other operators who wish to use parts of its network (BT plc. , 2012, section 5).

This method of charging sections of the organisation does have weaknesses. The results are not "costs" as usually understood. Rather they are target contributions required from organisational units if the organisation is going to recoup its original investment on the assumption that the plans at decision making time are realised. Their use may give rise to bargaining, gaming and possibly organisational conflict. This because individual units would argue that they should pay only the incremental costs they cause the organisation. In terms of Table 1 this would amount to units A, B and C covering only their variable costs whereas the centre would wish them to also cover the costs shared with other units (Sharkey, 1989, 35—42). Managers might find this approach difficult to understand.

This approach may seem rather abstract however the amounts of resources generating joint fixed overheads in the economy are increasing not only in the digital area but also wherever information and intellectual capital based resources are used. Developing some meaningful way of accounting for joint resources would seem fundamental with digital products. Currently the approach just discussed would seem the best available. This is an important but difficult area for future management accounting research.

4. Strategic management accounting

Dynamic and turbulent markets involve major changes in consumer and producer markets and therefore what has been called "strategic management accounting" (SMA) may offer current promise to practical accountants (Simmonds, 1981). This may also be the case for organisations that create and produce digital products. They need to attract vast number of customers and advertisers in an environment of very stiff existing and potential competition—we recall only the products which have been successful; most attempts fail. Here only a brief survey can be presented. Basically SMA offers a portfolio of techniques geared towards improving corporate strategy an area where at best accountants provide mainly accounting information (Hoque, 2006; Ward, 1997; Bhimani and Bromwich, 2010, 48—52).

Management accounting currently is rather internally focused being concerned mainly with the organisation's past costs, and seeking improvements in efficiency and planning over a relative short period. Advocates of SMA generally argue that accounting needs to look outwards into the market as this is where the consumers and the competition reside. As it stands SMA is a normative approach to management accounting in the sense it is based on a number of different analytical frameworks that are generally consistent in their recommendations but which have as yet have hardly been tested against empirical evidence.

SMA has a number of concerns. These include a wish to understand costs and their interactions with value drivers preferably over the life cycles of products and of strategies, seeking to determine the costs of implementing and carrying through strategies within firm and in comparison with competitors given an understanding of the organisation's cost structure and those of its rivals. Management accountants should focus on value-added relative to competitors, monitor performance in the market place covering the whole range of strategic variables over the long run.

The techniques which are usually seen as part of SMA include strategic orientated ABC, target costing, information on competitive positioning and competitive pricing and costing relative to competitors, life-cycle costing, quality costing, costing of the entire value chain and costing of the product attributes to the consumer (Guilding et al., 2000). All these techniques are of relevancy to the suppliers of digital products but the costing of product attributes and comparing these costs with the prices that consumers say they might be willing to pay for them may be of especial importance as may be the extension of this technique to costing the value drivers of advertisers.

The major research approach with SMA is the use of questionnaires to management asking them which of the techniques that usually form the basis of SMA they use and which they perceived to be of future value. Guilding et al. (2000) is perhaps the leading article which surveyed some of the largest companies in the New Zealand, UK and the USA. The response rates in the New Zealand and the UK were good but poor in the USA. They surveyed the use of 12 techniques. The results were poor, only strategic costing and pricing considering consumer view of attributes scored well for use but all the techniques except for one scored well in terms of perceptions of value. This suggests organisations are aware of these techniques. A more recent study of the largest Italian manufacturing firms (Cinquini and Tenucci, 2010) produced substantially higher results than in the Guilding et al. study and most used up to 10 of the techniques. Contrary to these results is a study of 116 German general hospitals that suggests that very few of these techniques were used (Lachmann et al. , 2013). This does suggest that there is a need to consider the possibilities of the differing use of SMA in different industries using SMA and perhaps even to consider the effects of the different cultures in different industries and even of national culture.

There is no doubt that the take up of SMA considered as the acceptance of the full bundle of SMA techniques is poor. Indeed the SMA brand name is not well recognised in practice. There are a number of definitions of SMA, different views as to the techniques that comprise SMA and different foci. Langfield-Smith (2008) is very critical but much of her evidence is taken from studies of ABC only some of which refer to its strategic dimensions. Against this many of the terms in the SMA lexicon have entered into practice, and SMA figures strongly in management accounting education and in consultancy. One area of research here is consider why in a dynamic and turbulent environment a set of techniques that seem to map into some of the problems of the environment seems not being utilised. It may be aspects of SMA are being used in the digital product industries as one might expect but there is as yet there is no evidence on this.

5. Conclusions

It has be argued here that most of the environmental changes considered here offer both opportunities and challenges to management accountants. In the earlier discussion of environmental changes some suggestions were made as to how management accounting could be adapted to help deal with such changes. Such suggestions are only propositions until subject to empirical evidence. Research should generate other options but case and field studies are urgently needed in this area as is survey based work.

When looking at digital products a number of problems that seemed to require amendments to the traditional cost structure model used by accountants were considered. With many such items the pricing of products is not necessarily closely related to their consumption or usage which is what conventionally is assumed to drive costs. In more extreme cases, consumption may be substantially divorced from the funding of production. The use of many search engines is free to consumers with the costs being recouped through advertising. The demand by advertisers may be only indirectly related to consumption of services by users. This requires rather a different modelling of revenue to that in the traditional model. Where the provider of digital products offers a number of services the organisation needs not only to seek to assign overheads to products but also revenues. Simple allocations of revenues, such as using the number of "hits" on advertisements, are likely to be arbitrary and not necessarily reflect the value drivers of those funding the services. It was said that care was required when seeking to determine the incremental revenue from a product or service.

Perhaps the major problem with digital products is the large up-front investments which are needed and which have the character that once the resources are provided they can be used for little or no cost to users. Thus such resources do not have a cost related to usage. A number of approaches to dealing with the costs of such resources were reviewed. None of these generate costs but rather seek to determine a charge on the user activities so that the costs of resources are recouped by the organisation. One possible approach which seems to make analytical sense and has been used in practice requires those parts of the organisation that use a resource together to provide sufficient revenue net of their other costs to pay for the resource. This area needs much more analytical research.

The article concluded by wondering why organisations facing environment changes do not seem to avail themselves of SMA. The techniques of SMA would seem often to map onto environmental changes.

References

[1] Atkinson, A. A. and Stiglitz, J. F. , 1980, *Lectures on Public Economics*, Maidenhead Berks: McGraw-Hill.

[2] Banker, R. D. , Ou, C. and Potter, G. , 1997, The compensating impact of strategic cost drivers in the US banking Industry, Working Paper, Temple University.

[3] Baumol, W. J. , Panzar, J. C. and Willig, R. D. ,1988, *Contestable Markets and the Theory of Industry Structure*, New York: Harcourt Brace and Jovanovich.

[4] Bhimani, A. and Bromwich M. , 2010, *Management Accounting: Retrospect and Prospect*, Oxford: CIMA Publishing-Elsevier.

[5] Bhimani, A. and Bromwich M. , 2009, Management accounting in a digital and global economy: The interface of strategy, technology and cost information, in Chapman, C. S. , Cooper, D. J. and Miller, P. B. (eds.) *Accounting, Organizations & Institutions*, New York: Oxford University Press, pp. 85—111.

[6] Bromwich, M. and Bhimani, A. , 1994, *Management Accounting: Pathways to Progress*, London: CIMA Publishing.

[7] Bromwich, M. and Hong, C. , 1999, Activity-based costing systems and incremental costs, *Management Accounting Research*, Vol. 10, No. 1, pp. 39—60.

[8] BT plc. , 2012, Primary accounting documents, available at: http://www.btplc.com/thegroup/regulatoryandpublicaffairs/financialstatements/2012/ primaryaccountingdocuments 2012.

[9] Cinquini, L. and Tenucci, A., 2010, Strategic management accounting and business strategy: A loose coupling, *Journal of Accounting and Organisational Change*, Vol. 6, No. 2, pp. 228—259.

[10] Cowen, T., 1992, *Public Goods and Market Failure: A Critical Examination*, New Brunswick, N.J.: Transformation Publishers.

[11] Economist, 2011, Capital Punishment-measuring the price of regulation, *Economist*, 10 September.

[12] Frontier Economics, 2012, A study investigating the extent to which there are economies of scale and scope in healthcare markets and how these can be measured by Monitor, Final report, August. Available from http//www. Monitor-nhsft. gov. uk/news-updates.

[13] Guilding, C., Cravens K. S. and Tayles, M., 2000, An international comparison of strategic management accounting practices, *Management Accounting Research*, Vol. 11, No. 1, pp. 113—135.

[14] Hallowell, R., 2002, Virtuous cycles: Improving services and lowering costs in e-commerce, HBS Note-802-169.

[15] Hippel von, E., 2005, *Democratizing Innovation*, Cambridge MA: MIT Press.

[16] Hoque, Z., 2006, *Strategic Management Accounting*, London: Butterworth-Heinemann.

[17] Lachmann, M., Knauer, R. and Trapp, T., 2013, Strategic management accounting practices in hospitals: Empirical evidence on their dissemination under competitive market environments, *Journal of Accounting & Organizational Change*, Vol. 9, No. 3, pp. 336—369.

[18] Langfield-Smith, K., 2008, Strategic management accounting: How far have we come in 25 years? *Accounting, Auditing & Accountability Journal*, Vol. 21, No. 2, pp. 204—228.

[19] Merchant, K. and Van der Stede, W., 2007, *Management Control Systems: Performance Measurement*, London: Pearson.

[20] Mueller, D. C., 2003, *Public Choice III*, Cambridge: Cambridge University Press.

[21] Panzar, John C. and Willig, Robert D., 1977, Economies of scale in multi-output production, *Quarterly Journal of Economics*, Vol. 91, No. 3, pp. 481—493.

[22] Panzar, John C. and Willig, Robert D., 1981, Economies of scope, *American Economic Review*, Vol. 71, No. 2, pp. 268—272.

[23] Sharkey, W. W., 1989, *The Theory of Natural Monopoly*, Cambridge: Cambridge University Press.

[24] Simmonds, K., 1981, Strategic management accounting, *Management Accounting*, April, pp. 26—29.

[25] Straub, D. W., 2004, *Foundations of Net-Enhanced Organizations*, Hoboken: John Wiley & Son.

[26] Teece, David J., 1980, Economies of scope and the scope of the enterprise, *Journal of Economic Behavior & Organization*, Vol. 1, No. 3, pp. 223—247.

[27] Ward, K., 1997, *Strategic Management Accounting*, London: Butterworth-Heinemann.

管理会计学刊　　JOURNAL OF MANAGEMENT ACCOUNTING STUDIES
第5卷　第1期　　Vol. 5, No. 1

业绩评价者评价行为及其影响因素研究

吴　革　陈晓泉*

摘　要　本文以综合业绩评价体系的使用为背景对我国业绩评价者做出评价决策的行为进行研究。结果表明：第一，受评价者行为影响，综合业绩评价体系的实施效果与理论预期有差距。第二，实验结果显示：(1) 业绩评价者使用综合业绩评价体系时偏好选择财务指标和共同性指标；(2) 在被提供更为详细的与战略有关的业绩信息时评价者选择关注共同性指标的程度降低；(3) 在给予更宽松的业绩评价时间时，评价者选择关注共同性指标的程度降低。第三，中国文化背景影响评价者的决策行为。

关键词　指标选择，评价者行为，综合业绩评价

一、引　　言

随着现代企业组织自身发展模式及经营环境发生巨大变化，企业业绩评价理论及实践方法也在持续改进发展。国内越来越多的企业借鉴或直接引入了包括平衡计分卡、业绩多棱体等综合业绩评价的思想，以期通过多类不同性质的指标科学、全面地衡量企业整体业绩。但这类多指标业绩评价体系在实施过程中除了受到企业经营目标及宏观环境等因素影响，评价者自身的知识结构、对战略的理解也会对体系的利用结果造成偏差。本文着眼于研究评价者对业绩评价方法的使用对评价结果产生的影响，运用心理学理论，将决策者认知和业绩评价相结合，采用实验研究方法比较在中国特殊的经济文化制度背景下评

---

*　吴革（通信作者），对外经济贸易大学国际财务与会计研究中心/商学院会计系教授，E-mail：wuugee@163.com；陈晓泉，新华通讯社，通信地址：西城区宣武门西大街57号，邮编100803，E-mail：tanya1988135@163.com。本文是国家社科基金项目“制度环境、会计准则国际趋同后果与资本市场监管体系创新”（批准号12BGL037）的阶段性研究成果。

价者在实施综合业绩评价中的决策行为,分析其影响因素。

二、文献综述和研究假设

(一)文献综述

评价指标、方法是评价过程中的重要方面,但并不是理论上完善的评价体系就等于客观合理的评价效果。认知心理学指出决策者的认知过程受其性格、知识、文化结构背景和环境的影响而做出不同的决策(何大安,2006)。管理心理学理论认为评价者拥有有限的认知和处理信息能力,指标过多、超过业绩评价者做决策所拥有的处理能力时评价不但不能改善业绩,反而会减少评价体系被期望具有的有效性。与"信息超载"直接相关的现象就是在面对多个指标提供的业绩信息时,评价者可能会选择性地关注企业在某些指标上的表现而轻视甚至忽略对企业业绩衡量同样重要的其他指标的表现,即存在认知偏见(cognitive biases)。Schiff and Hoffman(1996)通过实验证明了在对部门进行评价时,评价者倾向于使用财务指标,对经理人进行评价时则倾向于使用非财务指标。Frederickson et al.(1999)认为评价的结果导向的情况会因以前做出这类判断而在后来的决策中得到加强,作为长期使用的财务指标会持续被选择关注。另外一种指标选择现象就是对共同性指标的偏好。对这种现象的研究多集中于使用平衡计分卡(诺顿和卡普兰,2004)进行企业内部业绩评价。Slovic and MacPhillamy (1974)的实验结果显示业绩评价者在进行相似的任务时依赖于共同性和特殊性指标并赋予前者更高权重。Lipe and Salterio(2000)在平衡计分卡使用过程中也发现了该现象,这与平衡计分卡追求各方面平衡的初衷相悖。若独特性指标反映一个业务单元的关键层面,那么对这些指标的疏忽会削弱平衡计分卡作为战略管理系统的效用。Ittner,Larker and Meyer (2003)对全球财务公司GFS采用平衡计分卡红利计划的案例进行研究,由于分部经理抱怨评价指标偏好性以及计算奖励采用标准的不确定性,该公司最终取消了平衡计分卡计划,重新使用以利润为基础的评价系统,研究得出的结论是使用平衡计分卡进行业绩评价时对计分卡某一特定部分指标赋予不同权重的做法可能会对评价结果产生负面影响。Banker,Chang and Pizzini(2004)发现指标只要和企业战略联系紧密都将被评价者关注。Dilla and Steinbart(2005)指出对平衡计分卡理论和发展相关知识有所了解的评价者会同时使用共同性和独特性指标来衡量下级业绩表现和分配红利，但在做决策时更重视共同性指标。

何晴(2006)的结论是虽然集体决策下评价者对战略有更好的理解，但对指标偏好现象并无明显改善。陈晶、张朝宓和张宇(2007)将指标划分为结果性指标和前导性指标两大类，认为认知者和认知对象会对认知结果有所影响，但在不同情况下评价者都赋予结果性指标以更高权重，不会因为对平衡计分卡有更深认识而重视前导性指标。张禾等(2007)同样证明了共同性指标选择偏好在中国企业中的存在，并提出向评价者提供辅助性的补充图表资料能有效改善这种现象。

由于文化能够引导和制约特定群体成员的行为，针对中国实际进行研究时，需考虑文化对业绩评价活动产生的影响。霍夫斯泰德(2010)构建的国家文化模型中，研究了一些国家民族权力距离及对不确定性的规避程度等一系列因素。就权力距离而言，我国长期受到封建思想的影响，权力距离远高于西方国家，高的权力距离可能会阻碍基层工作人员参与到业绩评价系统的制定之中，由远离经营活动执行者的上层管理人员制定的业绩评价体系可能会由于本身不合理或者未能被基层工作人员理解而影响其评价效果的发挥。高的不确定规避性意味着管理者需要更明确、可靠的信息来进行业绩评价，相较于传统的财务类指标来说，其他维度的指标会被认为缺乏可信度。在对待共同性和独特性指标时也存在这样的情况，共同性指标被认为具有更多的信息含量。这也可以用 Holstrom and Milgrom(1991)对多任务的委托—代理问题的分析解释，如果代理人承担两种以上的任务，且不同任务之间具有替代性，在此情况下，假定某些任务及其成果相对可观察，另一些任务相对不可观察，那么代理人会在完成前一类任务上投放更多的时间精力，却往往忽略后一类任务。另外，从我国的市场环境来看，不同所有制形式的企业在同一个市场上相互竞争是一个较为明显的特点，国有企业与非国有企业业绩评价差异较为明显，将评价者依据其所属企业类型分为两类进行研究是必要的。与成熟的市场经济相比，中国的市场机制还不够完善，包括产品市场和资本市场在内的对企业业绩的显示机制没有充分发挥作用。我国证券发展时间较短，制度建设尚待完善，上市公司信息未能充分披露的现象大量存在，甚至有些公司操纵非财务信息以提升企业表现。股权结构不合理、外部监管不力、政府不恰当干预、提供审计服务的注册会计师缺失必要的独立性，这些都说明公司治理机制存在许多问题，影响非财务信息披露的可靠性和完整性，利用其作为业绩评价标准的作用受到制约。下文的分析结合这些特点进行。

（二）研究假设

心理学研究发现人们做决策时具有结果偏向(outcome bias)(Lipe,1993;Ghosh and Lusch,2000),以前做过的结果导向的决策会强化之后做决策时结果导向的程度。市场经济环境中,投资者创办企业在于追求利润最大化,建立在会计数据基础之上的财务指标与绝大多数企业的盈利目标直接相连,即使是兼具特殊功能的国有企业,实现更多的盈利仍是其基本目标,因此财务指标较早且更为普遍地被企业管理者和股东接受。在我国自市场经济体制建立之初,财务指标评价就产生了,即使业绩评价体系中引入了非财务指标,财务效益也始终处于核心地位。据此可推断,作为传统业绩评价指标,财务指标仍会被评价者给予较之于非财务指标的更多关注。所以,本文提出的第一个假设是:

假设 1 进行业绩评价时,评价者会更注重财务指标而忽视非财务指标。

依据平衡计分卡理论,平衡计分卡中的多个指标间具备逻辑关系。战略地图是能够帮助业绩评价者有效描述战略的工具,它以一页纸的形式将组织的重要战略目标及其因果关系直观、清晰地呈现,业绩评价者可以更系统、完整地了解熟悉企业制定的战略。由认知理论可知,图表更利于个体明确数据间的关系,以文字和图表相结合的形式表述概念可以加强个体对该概念的理解(Glenberg and Langston,1992;Wittrock,1974)。我们推断高层管理者在被提供组织战略地图和对战略进行详细文字描述的信息时,若能更好地理解指标结构、相互间因果关系以及独特性指标对战略目标起到的作用,他们更有可能全面理解评价指标,从而会更多地关注独特性指标。所以提出以下假设:

假设 2 拥有详细相关战略文字说明和战略地图的业绩评价者较之于仅被提供相对简略文字说明的业绩评价者在进行业绩评价决策时会给予独特性指标以更多关注。

时间压力对审计判断绩效有重大影响,尽管不同理论对压力与判断绩效间关系的解释不同,但从实验研究和调查问卷的结果可以发现过高的时间压力会降低审计判断绩效。多数企业评价周期为一年,也有一些企业的周期为一季或半年,更短的会每月进行,很多评价者在完成业绩评价任务时承担着时间压力。从关于时间压力与审计绩效判断关系的理论研究中我们可以推断时间也会对业绩评价决策的制定产生影响。Hambrick and Mason(1984)提出的高层管理理论认为环境中出现现象数量庞大且复杂程度较高(现象主要指在经济全球化和信息技术日新月异的情况下，企业应对竞争以求生存发展所面临的现象，会影响决策者们作出判断决策的各种内外部因素)，远在人们理解和处理的能力范围之外，决策者进行决策时会对信息有所筛选。为节省时间更快地做出判断，决策者习惯于关注对比性强的共同性指标以此来简化评价过程。由此我们可以得出推论：在一定范围内，高层管理者花在一项业绩评价决策上的精力和时间越多，他们越有可能更多地考虑到独特性业绩评价指标。据此，本文提出以下假设：

假设 3　承担较小时间压力的业绩评价者较之于承担较大时间压力的业绩评价者在进行业绩评价决策时会给予独特性指标以更多关注。

三、研究设计

(一) 研究对象及样本的选取

实验对象为对外经济贸易大学国际商学院 MBA 和 EMBA 学员。共发出 140 份问卷，取回 140 份，由于一些被试者在实验中的疏忽而做出相同业绩评价或漏答题目等导致 9 份问卷不符合要求，有效问卷为 131 份。131 位参与者中，有 63 位男学员，占总人数的 48%，被试者平均工作年限是 9.5 年，最长工作时间为 21 年，最短为 2 年。

(二) 实验方法及步骤

本文采用实验的方法收集数据来检验上述假设。首先，根据时间压力大小，将研究对象分为承受较大时间压力和承受较小时间压力两组。进行正式实验前，我们请 70 位对外经济贸易大学国际商学院会计系研究生(没有参与正式实验)随机分成三组(分别为 10 人、30 人、30 人)进行实验。第一组在无时间限制情况下完成任务，平均耗时大约为 35 分钟，然后以此为基础进行实验。第二组实验限制时间为 30 分钟，第三组为 40 分钟。实验后参与者按照－5(时间压力非常大) 到 5(时间非常充裕)的分值对是否有时间压力进行打分，二、三组的平均分值为－1.87、1.63，在 5% 的显著性水平上平均打分分别小于 0 和大于 0，我们可以简单认为在 30 分钟的时间限制下被试者较明显地承担着在有限时间内完成评价任务的压力，而在 40 分钟的时间限制下只承担相对较小的压力。其次，根据获得的关于企业部门的战略信息详略和是否被提供战略地图情况再分成两组：战略信息详细并有战略地图组和战略信息简略且无战略地图组。每组 35 人，具体实验分组如表 1 所示。

表 1　实验分组

	时间压力较小 A	时间压力较大 B
无详细说明 C	AC	BC
有详细说明 D	AD	BD

AC、BC 组的被试者只有相对简单的文字说明，AD、BD 组的被试者拿到较为详细的额外信息，除对任务案例的文字介绍外还有两部门的战略地图。图 1 是甲煤矿的战略地图。AC 与 AD 组需在 40 分钟内完成任务，BC 与 BD 组需在 30 分钟内完成。

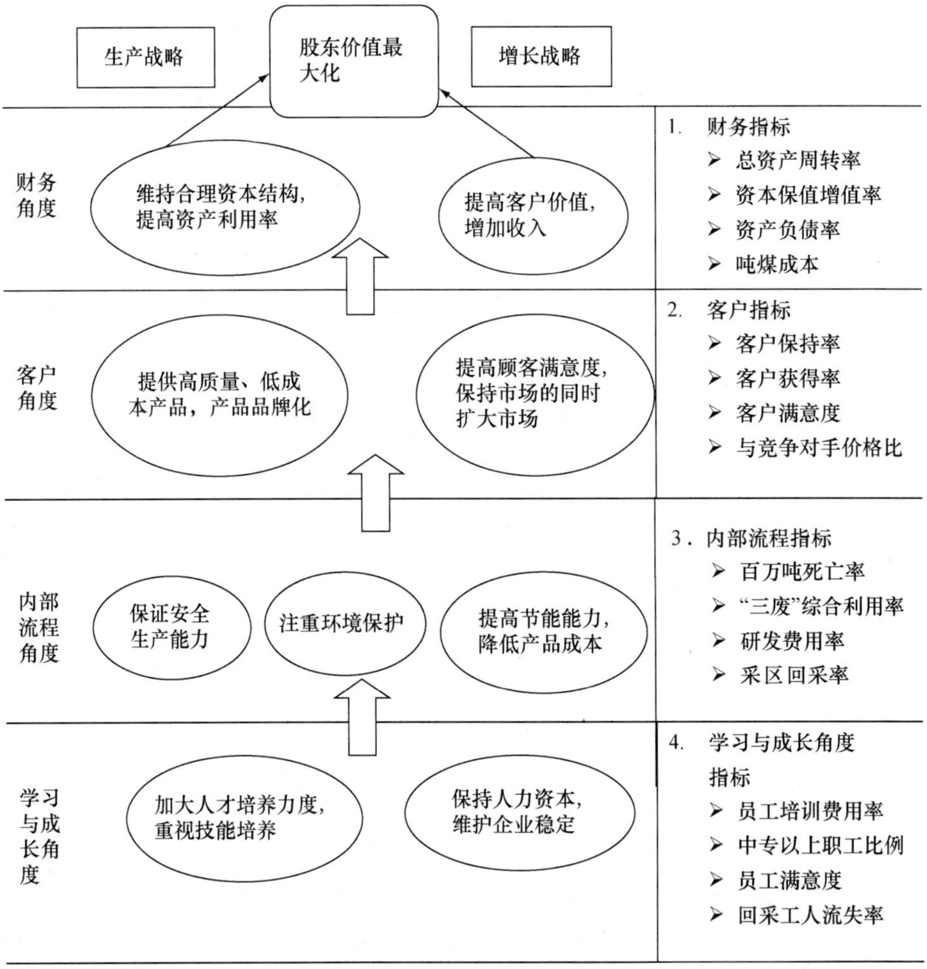

图 1　甲煤矿的战略地图

接着发放第二个文件夹，里面包括被试者需要完成实验任务的第二和第三部分的问卷。实验第二部分主要是对被试者构成进行统计，第三部分是被试者根据其对案例的体会，按照1(完全不同意)到7(完全同意)的评分标准给八句陈述打分，检验被试者对战略和整个实验的理解。第二、三部分问卷回答没有时间限制。

（三）实验基本情况

案例假设被试者是一国有煤炭企业A公司的高层管理者，对该公司甲、乙煤矿的经营业绩进行评价。AC与BC组得到的信息包括煤矿战略目标，各自的平衡计分卡，以及平衡计分卡中各指标的目标值和实际完成值。表2为甲煤矿的平衡计分卡。

本文参考Lipe and Salterio(2000)的实验设计加以调整改进，计分卡都包含四个维度共16个指标，每个维度中都有甲乙共同拥有的指标和分别反映各自目标战略的独特性指标。笔者认为，在没有一个事业单元明显优于另一个的情况下，使用一套平衡计分卡业绩报告就能完成实验要求。报告中除个别指标外，甲乙煤矿的实际表现均优于目标值，但甲煤矿在共同性指标上的表现都优于乙煤矿，在独特性指标上的表现则较之于乙煤矿差。为避免其他因素影响实验，两煤矿整体指标实际完成值超出目标值的比例基本一致。为避免被试者很快辨认出两份计分卡中相同的那些指标，大类中指标排序有所不同。计分卡没有给出明确的指标权重，这样有助于被试者对计分卡给出他们认为恰当的阐释。

表2　甲煤矿的平衡计分卡

评价指标	目标值	实际完成值	实际值优于目标%
财务指标			
1. 总资产周转率(次)	50%	53%	6.00
2. 资本保值增值率	100%	112%	12.00
3. 资产负债率	60%	57.7%	3.83
4. 吨煤成本	245	240	2.04
客户指标			
1. 客户保持率	100%	106%	6.00
2. 客户获得率	25%	27.8%	11.20
3. 客户满意度	83%	85.3 %	2.77

（续表）

评价指标	目标值	实际完成值	实际值优于目标%
4. 与竞争对手价格比	+2.3%	+2.38%	3.48
内部流程指标			
1. 百万吨死亡率	0	0	0.00
2. “三废”综合利用率	55%	59%	7.30
3. 研发费用率	0.4%	0.45%	12.50
4. 采区回采率	80%	83.83%	4.80
学习与成长角度指标			
1. 员工培训费用率	1.3%	1.42%	9.23
2. 中专以上职工比例	65%	70%	7.69
3. 员工满意度	70%	80%	14.28
4. 回采工人流失率	12%	11%	8.33

（四）变量设计

本文研究的因素变量有信息含量和时间压力，两变量均有两个水平，实验分组也是基于因素水平而设置：有详细说明和战略地图取值1，说明简略且没有战略地图取值0；承担较大时间压力取值1，承担较小时间压力取值0。本文将从业时间作为协变量进行方差分析，然后将被试者性别、评价经验、所在企业所有制性质及是否接触过煤炭行业相关业务作为控制变量在回归方程中进行进一步分析。其中，从业时间为问卷中被试者填写年数；性别男性取值0，女性取值1；评价经验通过被试者在以往工作经历中参与过人力资源管理、业绩评价、营销管理中的项目经验来衡量，有其中一项经验就得一分，没有相关经验得分为零；来自非国企的被试者取值0，来自国有企业的被试者取值1；在以前的工作经历中接触过与煤炭行业相关业务的被试者在此项取值0，其他取值1。

被试者首先对平衡计分卡的16个指标按照0（非常不重要）到5（非常重要）的标准打分。另外，要根据两座煤矿的业绩报告所提供的信息，分别对两座煤矿的业绩进行评价。评价标准为0表示业绩很差；20表示差；40表示较差；50表示一般；60表示较好；80表示好；100表示业绩优秀。因为对煤矿业绩评价涉及煤矿经营者的奖惩问题，故要求被试者对两个战略事业单元的评分不同，以甲乙得分之差作为分析的因变量。

四、研究数据及分析结果

（一）财务指标选择与综合业绩评价分析

表3显示按组别对不同类型指标重要性判定进行统计性描述分析的结果。从总体来看，对财务类指标的重要性评分3.99，高于对其他三类指标重要性评分的均值，内部流程类指标的评分为3.57，接下来分别是客户类、学习与成长类指标，评分分别为3.44和3.31。从提供信息和完成任务时间不同而分成的四组分别看，对财务类指标的重视情况都普遍存在。对共同性指标(3.64)和独特性指标的重要性评分(3.52)在总体上也有差别，但相比于对财务类指标的偏好程度较轻。

表3　指标重要性

指标类别＼组别		AC	BC	AD	BD	总体
财务类指标	均值	3.9833	3.9508	3.9886	4.0464	3.9933
	标准差	0.4545	0.3232	0.3663	0.3137	0.3631
客户类指标	均值	3.5792	3.3864	3.1515	3.6571	3.4437
	标准差	0.5614	0.5739	0.5985	0.4161	0.5691
内部流程类指标	均值	3.5333	3.3788	3.6250	3.7143	3.5658
	标准差	0.4912	0.4926	0.4273	0.4653	0.4807
学习与成长类指标	均值	3.4583	3.4280	3.2917	3.1036	3.3139
	标准差	0.4681	0.5135	0.4858	0.4808	0.5025
共同性指标	均值	3.6937	3.5928	3.5587	3.7054	3.6374
	标准差	0.3719	0.2928	0.3058	0.2744	0.3142
独特性指标	均值	3.5833	3.4792	3.4697	3.5554	3.5210
	标准差	0.3502	0.2714	0.2216	0.2323	0.2703

表4进一步比较了被试者认为不同类型指标对综合业绩评价的重要性是否有显著性差异。可以看出被试者对财务维度指标和内部流程指标的评分相对较高，尤其是对财务指标的重要性打分明显高于其他三类指标。在5%的显著性水平上对顾客类与内部流程类指标的打分均值无显著差异，但对内部流程类指标的打分均值要明显高于学习与成长维度，可能是评价者基于煤炭行业尤其注重安全生产和流程改进的特殊性。即便如此，财务类指标的评分还是明显高于内部流程指标的评分，显示出被试者对公司财务方面表现的重视，与假设1一致。

表 4　独立样本 t 检验

			方差方程的 Levene 检验		均值方程的 t 检验			
F			Sig	t	df	Sig(双侧)	均值差	
财务	客户	假设方差相等	16.081	0.000***	9.319	260	0.000***	0.550
		假设方差不等			9.319	220.782	0.000***	0.550
	内部流程	假设方差相等	6.466	0.012**	8.122	260	0.000***	0.427
		假设方差不等			8.122	241.894	0.000***	0.427
	学习与成长	假设方差相等	11.585	0.001***	12.544	260	0.000***	0.679
		假设方差不等			12.544	236.660	0.000***	0.679
客户	内部流程	假设方差相等	2.525	0.113	−1.877	260	0.062*	−0.122
		假设方差不等			−1.877	252.933	0.062*	−0.122
	学习与成长	假设方差相等	0.847	0.358	1.956	260	0.051*	0.130
		假设方差不等			1.956	256.075	0.051*	0.130
内部流程	学习与成长	假设方差相等	0.550	0.459	4.146	260	0.000***	0.252
		假设方差不等			4.146	259.492	0.000***	0.252

从上文对我国特殊背景分析可知，国企和非国企的业绩评价方式不同，管理者关注的业绩指标可能有所不同，本文将来自国有企业和非国有企业的被试者对指标主要是财务指标的重要性评分结果进行对比。表 5 显示来自国有企业的被试者为 79 人，占总人数的 60%，对财务类指标重要性评分的均值为 3.87，而来自非国有企业的被试者对财务类指标重要性评分的均值为 4.17。另外，来自非国有企业被试者对财务类指标评分的极大值和极小值均高于来自国有企业被试者的评分。表 6 说明企业性质对财务指标重要性评分均值有显著性意义。同时，来自不同企业类型的被试者在客户、内部流程及学习与成长这三类指标上的重要性评分并无显著差异，进一步证明了来自不同类型企业的被试者对财务指标的重视程度不同。

表 5　国有/非国有企业被试者财务指标评分对比

					均值的 95% 置信区间			
	N	均值	标准差	标准误差	下限	上限	极小值	极大值
国企	79	3.8750	0.36416	0.04097	3.7934	3.9566	3.00	4.63
非国企	52	4.1731	0.28022	0.03886	4.0951	4.2511	3.38	4.75
总数	131	3.9933	0.36305	0.03172	3.9306	4.0561	3.00	4.75

表 6　独立样本 t 检验

		方差方程的 Levene 方差					
		F	Sig	t	df	Sig(双侧)	均值差值
财务	假设方差相等	4.813	0.030**	5.005	129	0.000***	0.29808
	假设方差不相等			5.279	125.780	0.000***	0.29808

（二）共同性指标选择与综合业绩评价分析

表 7 是将实验总体按照本文分析的两个因素分成四组的描述性统计。四组被试者的从业时间在 9.5 年左右，平均评价经验得分约为 1.35，证实了实验随机分组的要求。两煤矿得分的最低值都是在 70 以上，说明他们的表现都超过了预计水平。四组和总体样本的甲煤矿得分的均值都显著高于乙煤矿得分的均值，由于报告中除个别指标外，甲乙煤矿的实际表现均优于目标值，但甲煤矿在共同性指标上的表现都优于乙煤矿，在独特性指标上的表现则较之于乙煤矿差，两煤矿整体指标实际完成值超出目标值的比例基本一致，所以在共同性指标上表现较好的甲煤矿的得分高于在独特性指标上表现较好的乙煤矿，这说明被试者在进行业绩判断时会在共同性指标上赋予更高权重，他们的决策行为具有共同性指标偏好。

表 7　分组描述性统计分析

分组		AC	BC	AD	BD
工作时间	样本量	$n=30$	$n=33$	$n=33$	$n=35$
	均值	9.667	9.606	9.364	9.486
	标准差	4.381 3	4.782 4	4.635 6	4.913 2
评价经验	均值	1.400	1.364	1.333	1.371
	标准差	0.813 7	0.783 3	0.919 3	0.877 4
甲煤矿得分	均值	88.367	91.727	86.970	86.514
	标准差	12.905 7	13.635 9	11.555 0	11.658 1
	最大值	94	97	94	95
	最小值	65	54	66	62
乙煤矿得分	均值	75.167	72.000	80.091	78.286
	标准差	11.728 5	10.152 0	9.326 8	8.893 4
	最大值	90	90	90	90
	最小值	60	50	60	60

表 8 是对甲乙分差进行的描述性统计分析，分析表明：从总体上看，全部被试者对两煤矿业绩评分的平均分差为 12.01，标准差为 4.068。在无详细说明和战略地图情况下，承担较小或无时间压力的分差均值为 13.20，承担较大时间压力的分差均值为 19.73；在有详细说明和战略地图的情况下，承担较小或无时间压力的分差均值为 6.88，承担较大时间压力的分差均值为 8.23；所以在实验提供可供参考的评价信息相同的情况下，被试者没有承担或承担较小时间压力时对两煤矿评分差距较小，承担较大时间压力时会给予甲煤矿以相对更高的评

分。另外，对均值的简单比较也说明在规定完成时间相同的情况下，被试者拥有详细说明和战略地图时对两煤矿评分差距较小，没有被提供详细说明和战略地图时会给予甲煤矿以相对更高的评分。从不同组别分差的极大值和极小值中可以看出，在只有简略信息且被要求在较短时间内完成任务的被试者业绩判断分差的极大值和极小值都相对较高。

表 8 甲乙分差的描述性统计分析

信息含量	时间压力	均值	N	标准差	极小值	极大值
说明简略	压力较小	13.20	30	4.189	−7	10
	压力较大	19.73	33	4.536	−5	15
	总体	16.46	63	4.522	−7	15
说明详细	压力较小	6.88	33	3.489	−5	10
	压力较大	8.23	35	3.524	−5	10
	总体	7.55	68	3.485	−5	10
总体	压力较小	10.04	63	3.810	−7	10
	压力较大	14.00	68	4.209	−5	15
	总体	12.01	131	4.068	−7	15

误差方差的齐性(Levene)检验(见表 9)表明：$F=0.343$，$P>0.05$，方差齐。表 10 的结果表明信息含量和时间这两个因素对评价结果的影响显著。因素信息含量：$F=4.145$，$P(\text{Sig}=0.044)<0.05$，可以认为信息含量这一因素对指标偏好影响显著，在信息含量充足(即被提供战略详细说明和战略地图)和信息含量相对缺乏两种情况下，评分分差的均值有显著性差异；因素时间：$F=4.304$，$P(\text{Sig}=0.040)<0.05$，可以认为时间压力这一因素对业绩评价的影响是显著的，在时间压力较小和较大两种情况下，评分分差的均值有显著性差异；因素信息含量×时间：$F=2.460$，$P(\text{Sig}=0.119)>0.05$，可以认为信息含量与时间这两个因素的交互作用不显著。协变量效应由被试者的从业时间决定，其对评分分差无显著影响。

表 9 分差的 Levene 检验

Levene 统计量	df1	df2	Sig
0.343	3	127	0.795

表 10　业绩评价方差分析

源	Ⅲ型平方和	df	均方	F	Sig
校正模型	172.975	4	43.244	2.754	0.031**
截距	372.074	1	372.074	23.693	0.000***
从业时间	0.343	1	0.343	0.022	0.883
信息含量	65.090	1	65.090	4.145	0.044**
时间	67.596	1	67.596	4.304	0.040**
信息含量×时间	38.627	1	38.627	2.460	0.119
误差	1 978.689	126	15.704		
总计	4 007.000	131			
校正的总计	2 151.664	130			

为了进一步验证假设 2 和假设 3，构造以信息含量和时间压力为自变量、评分分差为因变量的回归方程，将被试者的从业时间、评价经验、性别、所在企业所有制性质及是否接触过煤炭行业相关业务这些因素设置为控制变量进行分析。构造的回归方程如下：

$$P=\beta_0+\beta_1\mathrm{INFO}+\beta_2\mathrm{TIME}+\beta_3\mathrm{WKYR}+\beta_4\mathrm{EXP}+\beta_5\mathrm{SEX}+\beta_6\mathrm{TYPE}+\beta_7\mathrm{IND}+e \quad (1)$$

其中，P 是因变量，即被试者对甲乙煤矿业绩评价的分差；自变量为信息含量(INFO)、时间压力(TIME)，控制变量是从业时间(WKYR)、评价经验(EXP)、性别(SEX)、工作企业类型(TYPE)和是否接触过与煤炭行业相关业务(IND)；e 是误差项。

表 11　回归分析结果

	非标准化系数		标准系数	t	Sig	共线性统计量	
	β	标准误差				容差	VIF
(常量)	1.037	1.303		0.796	0.428		
INFO	−1.513	0.663	−0.187	−2.281	0.024**	0.980	1.020
TIME	1.332	0.657	0.164	2.027	0.045**	0.999	1.001
WKYR	0.036	0.077	0.041	0.474	0.636	0.855	1.170
EXP	−0.735	0.429	−0.152	−1.714	0.089*	0.829	1.206
SEX	0.167	0.663	0.021	0.252	0.801	0.980	1.020
TYPE	0.879	0.686	−0.106	−1.281	0.202	0.955	1.047
IND	3.377	0.927	0.300	3.642	0.000***	0.968	1.033
$R^2=0.194$，调整 $R^2=0.148$，$F=4.233$，$P<0.05$							

模型的判定系数 $R^2=0.194$，调整后 $R^2=0.148$。虽然判定系数不高，但 F 值为 4.233 且在 5％的显著性水平下显著，表明回归模型总体显著，模型成立且具有统计意义。另外，在此设回归模型的主要作用在于对变量间影响关系的检验而非方程拟合程度。Durbin-Watson 的值为 1.933，表明残差间相互独立无自我相关。VIF 值均小于 10，说明方程不存在多重共线性现象。

回归方程系数的 t 检验结果显示，信息含量、完成任务时间、被试者的行业工作经历这三个因素对业绩评价结果有显著影响。从业时间、性别、来自企业类型则对结果无显著影响（Sig＞0.05）。从自变量的回归系数可以看出，信息含量对于评分分差产生负方向的影响（回归系数＝－1.513，t＝－2.281，Sig＝0.024），也就是说，提供更为详细的战略信息可以帮助缩小评分分差，评分者相对于只有较少信息时会更多地关注到独特性指标，指标选择偏好的现象不是非常明显，这个结论验证了假设 2。时间压力对被试者对两煤矿业绩评价分差有正面影响（回归系数＝1.332，t＝2.027，Sig＝0.045），较大的时间压力会导致被试者赋予共同性指标以更高权重，而承担较小时间压力的业绩评价者较之于承担较大时间压力的业绩评价者在进行业绩评价决策时会给予独特性指标以更多关注，这个结论验证了假设 3。评价经验对评价分差有较弱影响（Sig＝0.089）。而从业时间对分差无显著影响，且从符号方向来看从业时间越长导致更明显的共同性指标偏好，与预期相反。

通过统计分析我们发现被试者普遍认为案例中对业绩指标的分类是合理的（平均得分为 5.221），根据战略的不同，两煤矿选取的业绩指标应该不同（平均得分为 4.04）。这些结果在不同分组间无明显差异。但拥有详细相关战略文字描述和战略地图的被试者能更好地掌握指标间的相互关系，深入理解煤矿经营情况和发展战略（平均得分为 5.4）并认为完成评价任务无太大难度（平均得分为 2.83）。在短时间内进行业绩判断、没有详细相关战略文字描述和战略地图的被试者理解较差（平均得分为 2.336），另外只有此组被试者认为评价任务的完成有一定难度（平均得分为 6.37），与其他组相差明显。

五、结 束 语

研究表明中国业绩评价者在进行综合业绩评价时其行为存在明显的指标选择偏好，评价过程中，评价者会更注重财务指标而忽视非财务指标；承担较小时间压力的业绩评价者较之于承担较大时间压力的业绩评价者在进行业绩评价决策时会给予独特性指标以更多关注；拥有详细相关战略文字说明和战略地图的业绩评价者较之于没有相关信息的业绩评价者在进行业绩评价决策时会给予独特性指标以更多关注；同时还发现来自非国企的管理者选择财务指标作为业绩评价依据的偏好更为严重，较多的业绩评价经验并没有明显改善指标选择的现象以及较长从业时间的被试者对业绩评价结果无明显影响。

本文还存在以下方面的局限性：第一，本文采用实验研究方法存在着本身固有的局限性，被试者不一定具有在煤炭行业工作的背景；第二，笔者自身能力有限，缺乏进行实验研究和在真实工作中进行业绩评价的经验，对于实验案例的设计还存在缺陷；第三，对时间压力的研究是本文的创新点，笔者通过正式实验前的测试确定了区分压力的时间限定，但并不十分准确；第四，抽样调查的统计调查方法存在误差；第五，本文在文字使用和体系框架的制定上还存在不足。

根据结论本文对中国企业的业绩评价提出以下几点对策建议：明确企业战略目标并做好目标的细分；依据企业实际情况制定合理的业绩评价体系，加强对员工相关教育培训；强化业绩评价者的理论认知，提供给评价者充足的信息，提高信息质量；完善评价程序，保障评价时间，建立责任制。

参考文献

[1] 戴唯·诺顿、罗伯特·卡普兰，2004，《平衡计分卡——化战略为行动》，广州：广东经济出版社。

[2] 何大安，2006，《选择行为的理性与非理性融合》，上海：上海人民出版社。

[3] 何晴，2006，通用性指标偏好及其实验研究——平衡计分卡在多部门企业中的应用，《清华大学学报》，第21期，第60—69页。

[4] 吉尔特·霍夫斯泰德，2010，《文化与组织：心理软件的力量》，北京：中国人民大学出版社。

[5] 张禾、曹建安、魏靓，2007，平衡计分卡指标偏见研究——基于企业内部组织单元绩效评价，http://www.docin.com/p-100950475.html.

[6] 张朝宓、张宇、陈晶，2007，业绩评价信息使用者的认知与判断——以平衡计分卡为背景的实验研究，《中大管理研究》，第12期，第22—46页。

[7] Banker, R. D., Chang, H. and Pizzini, M. J., 2004, Balanced scorecard: Judgmental effect of performance measures linked to strategy, *The Accounting Review*, Vol. 79, pp. 123—129.

[8] Dilla, W. N. and Steinbart, P. J., 2005, Relative weighting of common and unique balanced scorecard measures by knowledgeable decision makers, *Behavioral Research in Accounting*, Vol. 17, pp. 43—53.

[9] J. R. Frederickson, S. A. Peffer and J. Pratt, 1999, Performance evaluation judgments: Effects of prior experience under different performance evaluation schemes and feedback frequencies, *Journal of Accounting Research*, Vol. 37, pp. 151—163.

[10] Ghosh, D. and R. F. Lusch, 2000, Outcome effect, controllability and performance evaluation of managers: Some field evidence from multi-outlet business, *Accounting, Organizations and Society*, Vol. 25, pp. 411—425.

[11] Glenberg, A. and W. Langston, 1992, Comprehension of illustrated text: Pictures help to build mental models, *Journal of Memory and Language*, Vol. 31, pp. 129—151.

[12] Hambrick D. C. and Mason, P. A., 1984, Upper echelons: The organization as a reflection of its top managers, *Academy of Management Review*, Vol. 9, pp. 193—206.

[13] Holmstrom, B. and P. Milgrom, 1991, Multi-task principal-agent analyses: Incentive contracts, asset ownership and job design, *Journal of Law, Economics and Organization*, Vol. 7, pp. 24—52.

[14] Ittner, C. D., Larcker, D. F. and Meyer, M. W., 2003, Subjectivity and the weighting of performance measures: Evidence from a balanced scorecard, *The Accounting Review*, Vol. 78, pp. 725—758.

[15] Lipe, M. G., 1993, Analyzing the variance investigation decision: The effects of outcomes, mental accounting, and framing, *The Accounting Review*, Vol. 68, pp. 748—764.

[16] Lipe, M. G. and Salterio, S. E., 2000, The balanced scorecard: Judgmental effect s of common and unique performance measures, *The Accounting Review*, Vol. 75, pp. 283—298.

[17] A. D. Schiff and L. R. Hoffman, 1996, An explanation of the use of financial and nonfinancial measures of performance by executives in a service organization, *Behavioral Research in Accounting*, Vol. 8, pp. 134—153.

[18] Slovic, P. and MacPhillamy, D., 1974, Dimensional commensurability and cue utilization in comparative judgment, *Organizational Behavior and Human Performance*, Vol. 11, pp. 172—194.

[19] Wittrock, M., 1974, Learning as generative processes, *Educational Psychogist*, Vol. 11, pp. 87—95.

Research on Performance Evaluators' Behavior and the Influencing Factors

GE WU

(University of International Business and Economics)

XIAOQUAN CHEN

(Xinhua News Agency)

Abstract Through experimental methods, this paper aims at analyzing the evaluators' behavior while they are making the evaluation decisions, trying to find out the factors influencing the behavior. The main findings are as follows. Firstly, indices which measure the human capital and non-financial aspects are added into the comprehensive performance evaluation system. It is a big improvement compared to the traditional performance evaluation system. However, influenced by the evaluators' behavior, the effect of the application often can't meet the theoretical expectation. Secondly, the empirical results indicate that: (1) that Chinese evaluators prefer to choose the financial or common indices in the evaluating process; (2) the more detailed strategic information provided the lower extent of choosing part of the indices or overlooking the non-financial or unique indices; and (3) having lower time pressure to complete the evaluating task leads to the lower extent of choosing part of the indices in the comprehensive performance evaluation. Thirdly, the evaluators' behavior is affected by China's institutional background. Their index selection preference is obvious. The evaluators from the non-state-owned enterprises pay more attention to the financial indices. Additionally, longer work time or richer working experience can't effectively change the preference.

Key words Comprehensive Performance Evaluation, Index Selection, Evaluators' Behavior

管理会计学刊　　JOURNAL OF MANAGEMENT ACCOUNTING STUDIES
第5卷　第1期　　Vol. 5, No. 1

管理会计变革与创新的研究述评

周　琳　潘　飞　刘燕军*

摘　要　本文对管理会计变革与创新的理论基础和具有代表性的路径模型、过程模型、要素模型分别进行了详细的阐述与评价，指出了现有理论、模型的相互联系与区别、适用范围、不足之处等，在此基础上提出了我国未来研究的具体对策、建议。

关键词　管理会计变革，创新，模型

一、引　　言

管理会计变革(management accounting change)是企业为了适应内外部环境变化，对其管理会计系统进行调整、改变、创新，从而更好地实现组织目标的过程(Burns et al.，2001；Scapens，2006)。国外研究表明，管理会计创新在企业中被采纳和实施会使得原有的管理会计规则和惯例发生改变，引起组织结构、企业文化、相关利益群体的态度、人员行为的变化等，这些都会使管理会计创新在具体实施过程中变得复杂和不确定(Hopwood，1987；Libby and Waterhouse，1996)。这一主题日渐成为国外管理会计研究关注的重要领域，并取得了丰富的研究成果。研究人员运用不同的理论进行解释，提出了不同的变革模型，从不同角度和层次揭示企业管理会计变革与创新的过程与本质。

---

*　周琳（通信作者），河南财经政法大学会计学院讲师，E-mail：zhoulinzz@163.com，通信地址：河南省郑州市文化路80号，邮编：450002；潘飞，上海财经大学会计学院副院长、教授。E-mail：panfei@mail.shufe.edu.cn，通信地址：上海市杨浦区武川路111号，邮编：200433；刘燕军，英国纽卡斯尔大学商学院讲师，E-mail：y.j.l.liu@newcastle.ac.uk。本文为国家自然科学基金重点项目“以价值为基础、以战略为导向的中国企业管理会计研究”(项目号71032005)以及教育部人文社会科学重点研究基地重大项目“中国企业管理会计行为研究”(项目号10JJD630005)的阶段性研究成果。

我国学术界对于管理会计创新在企业的实施过程、遇到的问题、影响顺利实施的因素等重要问题探讨较少。与西方企业相比，我国企业具有截然不同的制度背景和企业文化。本文通过对已有相关研究进行系统梳理和详细评论，指出现有研究的不足，并对国内未来的研究进行展望。这将有利于我们考察我国企业管理会计变革与创新的过程，并赋予其丰富和独特的内容。

本文以下部分的结构安排如下：第二部分是管理会计变革与创新的理论解释；第三部分是管理会计变革与创新的模型述评；第四部分是总结与展望。

二、管理会计变革与创新的理论解释

已有研究从不同的层次和角度，用不同的理论对管理会计变革进行解释。在此，我们对这些理论进行阐述和简要评价。

（一）新制度社会学理论

新制度社会学理论（以下简称 NIS）主要关注组织与制度环境的相互影响，社会预期对组织的影响，以及这些预期被如何反映在组织实践和经营特征中（Martinez，1999）。依赖于社会学和组织学，新制度社会学理论已经越来越成为有生命力的解释个人与组织行为的理论。

以 NIS 为基础的会计方面的研究，主要关注组织外部的制度环境，即社会、经济和政治对组织会计实践的影响（Covaleski et al.，1993，1996；Carruthers，1995）；同时，也考察制度因素以及传统经济因素对理解管理控制系统变革的重要作用（Covaleski and Dirsmith，1988；Abernethy and Chua，1996；Burns and Scapens，2000；Collier，2001）。

NIS 主张考虑制度环境而不仅仅是技术环境的原因在于，组织易于受到法律或文化规则以及社会义务的影响（Scott and Meyer，1991）。对组织来说，它所处的特定行业构成了组织所面临的主要制度环境。例如，主要的供应商、资源、产品、消费者、管制层，以及其他提供相似服务或产品的组织等（DiMaggio and Powell，1983）。每一个组织都要遵守所在行业的规则体系，这些规则体系的具体体现"构成了社会现实"（Greenwood et al.，2002），产生了制度规则。

NIS 认为管理会计变革主要受到制度因素的驱动，而不仅仅是效率因素（Granlund，2001）。它强调组织采纳新的管理会计实践是为了更好的经营管理和在其行业内保持合法性(Covaleski et al.,1996)。也就是,组织并不仅仅为了资源和顾客而竞争,也会为了政治权力和制度合法性以及社会和经济适应性而竞争(DiMaggio and Powell,1983)。寻求合法性可能促使公司从形式上而不是从提高效率角度出发采纳新的组织结构和实践(Meyer and Rowan,1977)。这使我们可以将会计与控制系统看作"形式上合法"的工具。

由于NIS重视组织所处的外部环境及其对组织内部变革的影响,所以该理论会广泛应用"脱离"现象(decoupling)、"合法性"等概念来解释管理会计变革的过程及其变革本质(Scott,2001;Covaleski et al.,2003)。这类研究将"脱离"现象看作是组织对实施新的会计惯例的反应。通常认为,组织或者其关键决策制定者由于外部压力通过实施新的会计实践试图保护来自外部的合法性,但同时为了保持组织的技术效率而并没有真正在日常经营活动中实施这些新的组织实践。"脱离"现象也允许一定程度的抵制。例如,Dambrin, Lambert and Sponem (2007)深入考察了"脱离"现象,意味着"变革"并不总是真正改变组织行为者的日常经营活动。Moll and Hoque(2011)运用案例研究方法考察了一家澳大利亚大学如何为"成为一所重要的资金资助单位"而实施预算系统以保持其"合法"地位的持续的、充满争议的过程,这有助于我们理解会计是如何有助于保持组织的合法经营过程。作者认为经理人员、员工和其他内部相关者应该被视作重要的保持"合法性"的主体,但由于他们的价值理念及预期与该预算系统不一致,他们通过超支或结余花费动摇了预算的权威性。该文的核心贡献在于,不仅要关注来自外部管制者的制度要求,更要关注组织内部的制度需求。

NIS分析的层次是组织行业(Carruthers, 1995; Chua, 1995; Mouritsen, 1994)。并且,关注"趋同的变革",包括新的实践活动的传播过程或结果。另外,许多NIS在会计方面的研究,强调制度创新的"需求层面",而忽视"供给层面"(Scott,2001),尤其是忽视相关职业团体的制度化地位如何有助于他们传播新的会计实践(Meyer,1994)。

它忽视组织内部因素,尤其是忽视组织内部在面对一项管理会计创新的采纳和实施中的权力斗争、冲突和变革过程(Scott,2001);忽视新的管理会计实践如何在组织中生存和发展,将组织实践完全看作一个既定时间点的结果,而不关注与变革相关的动态过程或行为者发挥的作用,将组织看作一个整体、消极的实体或"黑匣子",仅仅符合环境要求就认为该项实践活动在组织中得到合法认可(Perrow, 1986; DiMaggio, 1988; Greenwood and Hinings, 1996; Scott, 2001;

Greenwood,et al.,2002)。这些导致对NIS的批评,认为NIS与权变理论类似(Zucker,1977)。

（二）旧制度经济学

旧制度经济学(以下简称OIE),始于19世纪末20世纪初,主张从社会制度发展的角度论述制度结构和制度变革,强调制度在社会经济生活中的决定作用和对个人行为的影响。

旧制度经济学通常将制度定义为“一种普及性和永久性的思想或行为方式,体现在一个群体的习惯或一群人的风俗中”(Hamilton,1932)。制度往往是指机构或组织,如公司、工会、家庭等,不仅指机构或组织的有形内容,而且还包括无形内容,如所有权、集团行为、社会习俗、生活方式等。Veblen(1989,1918)拿生物基因进行类比,强调制度往往比生物基因更可塑,但也会以不同方式发生突变。在对制度变革的分析中,Veblen认为思想和行为的新方式来自“懒惰的好奇”(idle curiosity),即人类倾向于实践和创新,导致新技术的产生,并及时支持固定的行为模式。因此,尽管Veblen一直强调人类行为受到习惯倾向的影响,但是他的“懒惰的好奇”概念将创造性和新颖性引进这个过程。所以,制度的变革和稳定并不是孤立的,它们是同时进行的同一过程的两个方面。

OIE尤其适合于研究制度变革,其关注的焦点是组织的惯例及其制度化,以及组织惯例的变革过程,例如管理会计变革。因此,OIE适合于解释组织内部的管理会计变革过程。

OIE适合于考察形式上的变革,以及会计变革的路径依赖本质。它使我们能够关注“稳定”和“变革”之间的关联。“稳定”与“变革”以一种相互依赖的关系交织在一起。正如Granlund(2001)运用Gidden的结构理论解释管理会计系统内部和外部的稳定性,并号召要更多地分析管理会计实践的变革与稳定,以便这些对立的力量及其相互关系能够更好地被人们理解。例如,Siti-Nabiha and Scapens(2005)的研究发现“稳定”和“变革”不一定是对立的或相反的力量,而是在不断进化的变革过程中交织在一起。

根据OIE方面的文献总结出三种制度变革分类,有助于我们理解管理会计变革过程。这三种分类提供了划分与区别不同种类变革过程的方法,分别是:第一,正式和非正式的变革,即有意识和无意识的变革。通过有目的的设计,通常是引进新的规则或有权势的个人或团体的行为，正式的变革得以发生。这种正式的管理会计变革，可能会比试图改变体现在公司现有管理会计惯例中的思维方式更直接。但是，这种正式变革的成功实施需要企业成员不断接受新的思维方式(Burns and Scapens，2000)。如果缺乏相应的思维方式变革，只是形式上发生了正式的变革过程，那么在变革实施过程中就可能出现问题。例如，延缓、阻碍变革的行为，以及担忧和抵制的情况就会出现，可能导致变革的失败。

第二，革命式和进化式的变革，即根本性的变革或逐渐的变革。革命式的变革使得现有惯例和制度发生根本性的改变，而不断演化的变革是逐渐进行的，仅仅对现有惯例和制度有较小的破坏。它们和有意识与无意识的变革的区别存在一些相似之处。管理会计中有意识的变革可能根源于现有的惯例和制度，因此是进化式的变革，而不是革命式的变革。然而，以非正式过程进行的无意识变革本质上可能是革命式的，因为它们能够挑战现有的制度。

第三，倒退式和前进式的变革，即有价值的和形式上的变革。有价值的变革主张将最好的知识与技术应用到解决问题上，而形式上的变革并没有引起企业相应问题发生实质性的改变，主要是保护现有的权力结构。这种分类有助于我们加深对管理会计变革的了解。前进式的变革行为能够在保持组织原有形式和状况下发生，因为新发明的或产生的技术能够使人们对原有占据主导地位的行为价值产生疑惑。这种分类也有助于使研究人员开始对以下问题提出疑问：一个组织的管理会计惯例是否大部分是形式上的，因此保护既定利益团体的权力和利益，并潜在阻碍新的实践活动的发展，包括新技术的引进和应用以及研发的投入？最后，这种分类也有助于我们对企业现有的管理会计惯例和制度提出质疑，这需要关注其所处的制度环境，进而有可能在各种条件具备时进行有价值的改革。

（三）行为网络理论

行为网络理论(以下简称 ANT)是一种旨在理解变革和规则的理论(Monteiro and Zanjacomo，2000)。ANT 最初是 Latour(1987)和 Callon(1986)在科学技术研究领域的研究成果，主要关注社会运行是如何实现的。它不是将社会看作由静止不动的实体和结构所组成，而是将人类和非人类的行为者理解为相互影响以创造社会环境的实体。

该理论随后被许多以过程为导向的信息科学研究者借鉴(Boland，1996；

Quattrone and Hopper,2001),而且已经被用来研究会计变革(Chua,1995;Miller,1991)。ANT关注不同类型因素对会计变革的作用。例如,它关注ABC作为一种实践,在实施过程中被社会化、组织化和技术化的方式。研究思路是通过考察不平等的、不同种类行为者的积极选择和权威专家、咨询师等在临时稳定的跨组织网络中发挥的作用来解释会计变革。它可以用来论证不同机构、组织行为者和咨询师构成的网络如何能够改变一个组织的会计和生产活动。同时,它也关注不同类型的行为者发挥的作用,即能够作为稳定和调和不同行为者的机制。这有助于我们理解会计变革是如何发生的,或更精确地说,变革是如何在组织中实施的。

创新传播理论认为新的技术一旦被证明是有效的、最好的实践,或与权势集团的目标相一致,就会在组织之间传播使用,即完全是由社会因素决定的(Latour,1987)。然而,Latour认为一种技术的成功或失败不可能被一系列社会因素预测(例如,国家机构与行业资本的结合,会计师事务所和会计准则制定者的联合等),其命运取决于发明者之后采纳实施的组织,其成功或失败由许多不同的人为因素、非人为因素所决定。并且,传播意味着在随后的采纳中被复制,而环境的特殊性常常会导致重要的改变和修改。例如,公司A和B都认为它们实施了ABC系统,但是由于公司的机制不同,因此,它们会对ABC进行相应的调整以适应各自的实际情况。

ANT主要是从"供给层面"对创新技术的传播进行理论解释,尤其是关注职业的制度化地位是如何有助于他们传播新的会计实践(Meyer,1994)。例如,促使管理会计创新的使用成为一种时尚的主体包括咨询公司、早期采纳者以及会计学术界(Abrahamson,1991;Granlund and Lukka,1998;Malmi,1999;Innes et al.,2000;Armstrong,2002;Jones and Dugdale,2002;Carmona and Gutierrez,2003)。

Jones and Dugdale(2002)考察了管理咨询师和哈佛学术界是如何促使ABC为不同团体,尤其是关键的学术团体和咨询界人士所需要。咨询师是重要的中介力量,因为其在全球范围内拥有丰富的会计专业知识和实践经验。他们担任不同企业的管理顾问,这增强了其影响力,因此,管制者对其赋予外在合法性,公司也听从他们的建议(DiMaggio and Powell,1983,1991)。Hopper and Major(2007)论述了采纳ABC的益处,以及国家、政府和咨询师在其中发挥的作用。

也有文献以 ANT 为基础，检验了管理会计变革作为一个“加工”过程，不同的组织利益和各种社会、政治、经济因素对这个过程的影响(Chua，1995；Preston et al.，1992)。

Briers and Chua(2001)采用实地研究，对 ABC 在一家澳大利亚铝厂的实施过程进行研究，运用 ANT 理论考察行为者网络和不同的参与对象在管理会计变革过程中发挥的作用。作者认为会计变革受到组织内和组织外因素的影响。主要利益相关者的利益和信念(Palepu，1987)，经济命令式的权力，权势群体的愿望、信念和价值以及变革的环境很明显都会在会计变革中发挥作用(Ezzamel and Bourn，1990；Dent，1991)，但这些仅仅是众多因素中的一部分。ABC 被采纳并不是因为大家一致认为它有很好的战略适应性或它给公司带来多大的效用，这种解释在某种程度上太理性或太客观。作者认为，各种各样的行为者和行为体(本土人员和咨询师，人为因素和非人为因素)导致了变革的发生，每一类因素都在尽力构建较强的网络，以加强他们对 ABC 的支持和实施。这篇文章考察了 ABC 作为一种实践，被社会化、组织化、技术化的方式，为我们提供了一种分析工具，有助于我们理解会计变革是如何发生的，或更精确地说，变革是如何在组织中实施的。

(四) 组织变革理论

组织变革(以下简称 OC)是组织科学领域的重大研究课题，变革已经成为组织的一个重要组成部分，组织来源于变革，并在变革的过程中不断更新、完善，并重新生成自我。Pettigrew et al.(2000)等认为围绕着组织变革与发展而形成的新的研究是组织科学自 20 世纪 80、90 年代以来最具挑战性意义的一个研究领域。组织变革作为经济管理领域中的一个重要议题，更是受到了战略、组织结构、人力资源管理和组织行为等不同研究领域和国内外学者的广泛关注和研究。

OC 相关研究经历了几个主要阶段。20 世纪企业组织变革的主题沿着结构变革——文化变革——流程变革的轨迹进行。近年来，更多学者从实践中发现，单一内容的变革并不能满足企业的需要，正如 Pasmore et al.(1992)指出，虽然流程很重要，但结构、文化、关系和目的的改进也决定了企业的价值，这种价值体现在质量、服务、成本、速度和创新等五个方面。

从研究主题来看，国外有关 OC 的研究多集中于以下几个方面：组织变革的背景或动因（组织外部剧烈变化的环境），变革的模型（渐进模型、动态均衡模型和连续变革模型）、方式及方法（计划方法和突变方法），变革的趋势与内容（结构、人员、技术与文化等），变革的路径选择，变革的过程控制，变革的绩效衡量，管理与领导变革，变革的成功与失败等（李作战，2007）。

其中，对组织变革过程研究的关注和梳理，使我们对组织变革研究现状形成主线明晰的完整体系（高静美等，2010）。这类文献主要涉及与组织变革过程紧密联系的三个重要方面：一是组织成员对于组织变革的态度，尤其是抵制态度（Piderit，2000）。二是组织变革是否具有持续性（Buchanan，et al.，2005）。持续性方面的组织变革过程源于贯彻和扩散，并伴随着绩效提升。这一观点将影响持续性的因素分为个人、管理、文化和过程四类。Dale et al.（1997）研究了全面质量管理的持续性就是质量增长的保持过程，基于此提出了影响全面质量管理持续性的五个要素，即内外部环境、管理风格、政策、组织结构和变革过程。三是组织变革的关联性，即前面的变革是否会影响后续的变革（Beck，et al.，2008）。变革会增加进一步变革的可能性，所以变革被看作一个自我强化的过程，这个观点被称为“惯性假设”。

Pettigrew et al.（2000）认为，组织变革研究应该关注的六个关键性问题仍不完善，亟待改进。这些问题是：从多重情景和分析层次对组织变革进行分析和检验；将时间、历史、过程和行为纳入考察范围；同时考察变革过程与组织绩效结果；开展国际化和跨文化的比较研究；对可接受性、个性化发展、时序性、变革步伐以及偶发性与持续性变革展开研究；加强学术界和实业界的合作。

由于组织变革领域不仅会涉及组织政治学、制度经济学、心理学、行为学等社会科学，而且也包括混沌理论、信息化等自然科学的研究成果，因此在研究方法上呈现多样性，大致可分为以下几类：一是通过文献梳理的方法对组织变革领域不同研究方法及其背后的基本假设进行探讨；二是运用案例分析方法，进行较为深入、细致和典型性的分析；三是运用大样本实证分析的方法对组织变革领域的某一具体研究主题进行探讨，其研究结论的信度和效度较高。

在知识经济社会这种大的国际环境变化背景下，国内一些研究者从信息技术、知识经济、电子商务等对组织的宏观环境、产业环境以及组织内部的各级部门等各个层面所可能引发的变革问题进行了探讨。尤其是中国经济转型这个特定的历史阶段和背景下企业所必须实现的转变、医疗体制改革等政策性挑战所可能带来的医疗供应链管理的变革问题，以及国有企业改制的组织动因、环境约束与变革策略等相关问题都引起了国内学者从不同层面进行了诸多探讨和研究。

但是,国内组织变革研究更多地集中于对企业外部环境的分析及外部环境变化可能对企业的组织形态、运作方式和管理模式的影响,即趋势研究。这些趋势研究多集中在变革的组织结构和技术层面,而对具体变革方式、过程、内容和管理的研究则比较少。并且,我国在组织变革方面研究的主要问题是缺乏实证研究。多数文章局限于定性的描述变革的趋势,也就是关心目标,而不考虑过程与结果。但随着越来越多的企业进行各种变革而遇到实施困难,越来越多的国内学者开始关注变革过程和变革中的行为。

（五）理论评述

综上所述,NIS主要停留在宏观层面(Hasselbladh and Kallinikos,2000),关注的是管理会计创新传播模型,在用于理解那些不能纯粹由效率原因进行解释的变革方面非常有帮助。但是,NIS并不能真正地解释制度变革在组织内部实施的过程(Siti-Nabiha and Scapens,2005),所以它并没有为研究管理会计变革提供一个完美的和绝对独一无二的验证框架。

OIE对于解释组织层面是合适的,并且解释能力显著强于绝大多数以新古典经济理论为基础的会计研究(Scapens,1994)。但是,它在解释影响和决定组织环境的较高层次的社会、政治和经济问题方面存在局限性;并且,它不能解决组织行为如何影响整个组织行业或整个社会制度。

ANT主要是从创新传播的“供给层面”进行理论解释。例如,促使管理会计创新的使用成为一种时尚的主体包括咨询公司、早期采纳者以及会计学术界。权威专家、咨询师、企业内部不同利益群体参与者构成了跨组织网络。通过这些行为者在此网络中的积极行动和发挥的作用来解释会计变革,从而可以论证这种跨组织网络如何能够改变一个组织的会计和生产活动。

OC方面的研究与其他研究变革过程的观点相同,例如,都强调研究变革的过程、内容、政治和环境的重要性;对员工抵制变革的研究都是组织变革和管理会计变革理论和实践中的热点问题等。但是,考察组织变革的研究者通常使用“文化”这一概念(Bhimani,2003)。这里“文化”一词与OIE理论中“制度”的概念类似。然而,“文化”的含义更广泛。在研究管理会计变革时通常使用“制度”一词,因为“制度”一词与管理会计实践作为组织惯例有紧密联系。并且,大多数制度理论文献，往往更加关注微观层次、较短时期和逐渐发生的变革过程。

基于以上分析，我们用表1对管理会计变革相关的理论所涉及的关键问题进行汇总。

表1　理论解释比较分析

理论 项目	NIS	OIE	ANT	OC
分析层次	组织行业	单个组织	单个组织或组织行业	组织所处的宏观环境、产业环境以及组织内部的各级部门等各个层面
关注焦点	组织与制度环境的相互影响	组织的惯例及其制度化	社会运行如何实现，人类和非人类行为者如何相互影响以创造社会环境	主要关注变革过程的三个方面：组织成员对组织变革的态度，尤其是抵制态度；组织变革是否具有持续性；组织变革的关键性
会计方面的研究	主要关注组织外部的制度环境对会计实践的影响，强调制度创新的"需求层面"	适合于考察形式上的变革，以及会计变革的路径依赖本质	主要从"供给层面"对创新技术传播进行理论解释，尤其关注外界职业界如何有助于他们传播新的会计实践	在会计方面的研究比较少，多关注战略、组织结构、人力资源管理和组织行为等方面
针对管理会计变革的研究	主要受到制度因素的驱动，而不仅仅是效率因素。关注管理会计创新传播模型	适合于解释组织内部的管理会计变革过程，关注"稳定"与"变革"之间的关联性	关注管理会计实践被社会化、组织化和技术化的方式。各种各样的行为者和行为体如何导致了变革的发生	少量的研究会运用组织变革的框架研究管理会计变革

三、管理会计变革与创新的模型述评

依据不同的理论基础和视角，现有管理会计变革研究者提出了不同的理论模型，可以分为路径模型、过程模型和要素模型三类。其中，路径模型是从变革的路径角度来构建理论模型，如Burns and Scapens(2000)的制度演化模型、Dillard et al. (2004)的多层次制度化模型；过程模型是将整个变革过程划分为不同的阶段并探讨各阶段的影响因素，具有代表性的是Cooper and Zmud(1990)的六阶段模型、Anderson(1995)的修正六阶段模型；要素模型是以变革过程中的基本要素为框架建立理论模型，比较典型的是Innes and Mitchell(1990)的三要素模型、Cobb et al. (1995) 的三要素扩展模型、Kasurinen(2002)的三要素修正模型。各模型及其依据的主要理论基础如表2所示。

表 2 管理会计变革模型及其理论基础

管理会计变革模型		理论基础
路径模型	Burns and Scapens(2000)的制度演化模型	OIE
	Dillard et al. (2004)的多层次制度化模型	NIS
过程模型	Cooper and Zmud(1990)的六阶段模型	OC,信息系统实施
	Anderson(1995)的修正六阶段模型	OC,ANT,创新技术传播,信息系统实施
要素模型	Innes and Mitchell(1990)的三要素模型	系统理论
	Cobb et al. (1995)的三要素扩展模型	
	Kasurinen(2002)的三要素修正模型	

（一）管理会计变革的路径模型述评

Nelson and Winter(1982)认为,研究管理会计变革过程要求将新的会计实践随着时间变革的方式进行路径化。这里值得详细回顾和评述的是 Burns and Scapens(2000)和 Dillard et al. (2004)的模型,它们都以制度理论为基础,从不同层次对管理会计或制度的变革过程进行了理论描述和抽象概括。

1. Burns and Scapens(2000)的制度演化模型

该模型借鉴 Barley and Tolbert(1997)以及 Giddens(1984)的研究,以旧制度经济学(OIE)为理论基础,主要从组织层次,通过将管理会计变革理解为组织规则和惯例的变革进行分析,并运用制度理论发展出一个概念化管理会计变革的框架。

该模型对行为和制度进行区分,认为管理会计变革本质上是一种制度演化,其演化路径表现为制度与行为交互作用下的渐进模式,并且由规则和惯例通过"转化、实施、复制"过程将这两个领域联系起来。

"转化、实施、复制"过程主要包括四个过程。第一个过程反映各种既有制度借助权力结构、价值观等手段表征为管理会计系统中的种种惯例,这些惯例通过其社会意义、价值、权威的示范,对新规则(试图实现的变革目标)的影响十分长远。第二个过程反映规则和惯例对管理会计系统中各种行为的规范,即转化为具体的日常活动。新的规则和惯例的实施可能易于受到抵制,尤其是对既有的价值观构成挑战,并且行为者有充足的权力资源干预这一过程。第三个过程反映新的规则和惯例在多种场合下被复制,即它所规范的日常管理和经营活动或行为反复发生。第四个过程反映规则和惯例的制度化过程。制度脱离于它们特定的历史环境,是行为者对"做事情的方式"的理解、积累和表述。只有当新的规则和惯例蕴含的基本原则、原理在长期的潜移默化中植入人们的头脑中，并且被视为理所当然的做事情的方式时，新规则的制度化过程才宣告完成，这也意味着变革取得了成功。制度随后又转化为正在执行的规则和惯例，又形成新的规则，如此循环往复，等等。

该模型认为，在研究管理会计变革通过何种方式影响组织行为时，要充分认识到变革过程中权力发挥的作用以及对变革抵制的现象。因此，管理会计变革的核心问题在于能否实现"制度化"，即将变革目标由"规则"转化为企业持续运用的知识、技能，进而成为所有成员共同认可的决策与控制的惯例模式。

为了理解复杂的管理会计变革过程，必须明确组织规则和惯例代表了一种制度和组织成员日常的行为标准。尽管可能认为关注惯例是对研究变革的一种对立，但稳定和变革并不是互相排斥的过程，它们同时存在和发生。Lukka (2007)依据该模型，将组织决策制定有关文献中的概念"松散的连接"引入模型进行整合。作者考察了管理会计的"变革"与"稳定"，组织经营活动的"正式"和"非正式"方面。同时，作者尤其关注正式的规则和非正式的惯例之间的"松散的连接"关系，以及这种关系在理解管理会计变革与稳定方面发挥的作用。

尽管BS模型关注内部制度，即组织内理所当然的假定，但它也承认外部制度的重要性，以及来自组织外的制度变化压力。

该模型能使我们更好地理解组织内部管理会计变革的过程。并且，为了理解制度化过程在不同时期的特征，以及管理会计规则和惯例持续积累的过程本质，需要长期考察组织内的管理会计变革过程，并且需要将此过程定位在制度的时间和空间上。通过这类研究，研究人员和实务工作者将能更好地预测在管理会计变革中可能遇到的问题和困难。另外，将管理会计理解为组织规则和惯例，能够使研究人员关注管理会计思想、概念、技术、系统等，具有实践意义。

2. Dillard et al.(2004)的多层次制度化模型

该模型以社会理论为基础，对制度理论加以扩展，将制度理论和结构理论相结合，发展了一个递归(recursive)的制度化模型。它更注重过程，而不是结果，从而描述了持续的动态变革过程以及社会经济、政治因素在制度化建立、转变和瓦解中的显著影响。

该模型认为实践活动的制度化、转变和制度化瓦解是连续和动态的。该模型通过社会历史关系的三个层次(Weber，1958)，以一种层层串联的方式展示了制度化过程(Clegg，1989；DiMaggio and Powell，1983)。处于顶端的经济和政治层次建立了普遍的、广泛的理所当然的标准，这些标准被传播到组织行业层次，并被转化成更加具体、明确的实践和立法依据，用来评价组织层次的执行情况。对于组织来讲，重要的资源配置制度存在于组织行业层次。然而，组织可能是改革者（它在组织行业标准和实践前提下制定新的组织实践规则）或者是随后的采纳者（它复制创新者的实践，尽管有时是形式上的）。新的创新实践在组织之间或向较高层次发展推进，进而修改法定的实践和标准。在组织行业层次，合法和可接受的实践标准的变革通常反映了社会标准的变革。它们逐渐加强修订或减弱了广泛的实践和标准，但是偶尔会引起革命式的变革。政治和经济层次权力和意识形态的转变可能会引起组织行业层次规则和实践向下的变革。不同的行为者影响不同层次制度实践的实施。例如，政府官员、监管者和立法者处于政治经济层面；行业领先者、商业协会、外部咨询师处于组织行业层次，经理人员和工人处于组织层次。然而，层次之间持续的反复过程会发生向上和向下的变革，尽管通常存在足够的稳定性因素来限制实践的发展。

该模型包括了最近新制度经济学（NIS）提出的解决会计研究中的问题，尤其解决了 NIS 是如何忽视制度化实践的建立、传播和变革过程，以及人类权力、社会、经济和政治环境如何影响制度化实践。它更全面地表达了制度化过程，有助于更好地理解制度、会计实践和变革过程。

综上所述，路径模型是从变革的路径、机制角度来构建理论模型。路径模型的最大贡献在于将新兴的社会学理论和经济学理论引入管理会计研究，不仅弥补了传统管理会计研究主要以新古典经济学和新制度经济学为理论依据、只能寻找最优的“静态均衡”，却无法解释动态变革进程的不足（Burns and Scapens，2000），而且它指出变革的核心在于使新的管理会计规则“制度化”，这就阐明了变革的内在机理，打开了变革过程的“黑箱”。

（二）管理会计变革的过程模型述评

自从传统成本系统成为企业采纳先进制造方法的障碍而受到批评之后不久，研究人员开始讨论管理会计系统的变革过程、实施阶段以及对组织的影响。

1. Cooper and Zmud（1990）的六阶段模型

早期 IT 实施方面的研究认为，IT 实施的成功是由技术或组织因素决定的。这些研究忽视了决策制定过程，以及通常有助于 IT 实施的权力因素。随后的研究发现 IT 实施失败既不是技术原因，也不是组织原因，而是来自社会—技术因素之间的复杂交互作用，这些对组织实施变革是至关重要的（Bostrom and Heinen,1977;Kanter et al.,1992)。并且,这些研究认为新系统的成功实施需要组织有能力接受潜在的破坏性的变革。

Kwon and Zmud(1987)对 Lewin(1952)提出的组织变革三阶段模型进行了完善,将实施过程概括为六个连贯阶段(时间上会有重叠),即发起、采纳、适用、接受、惯例、融合。Cooper and Zmud(1990)借鉴 Kwon and Zmud(1987)的"信息系统实施模型",用这六个连贯的阶段来反映企业实施某种管理会计创新的变革过程。该模型每个阶段的主要任务和特征如表 3 所示。

表 3　Cooper and Zmud(1990)六阶段模型的特征

	主要任务	主要标志
发起阶段	变革的压力来自外部竞争或内部需求,积极或被动地寻找解决方案	确定解决方案
采纳阶段	变革的具体目标和方案在企业内部达成一致;投入必要的资源以利于变革的实施	投入必要资源以利于实施
适用阶段	新技术在企业中被开发、维护;对组织成员进行培训;对系统缺陷进行完善	新技术可以在企业中使用
接受阶段	新的管理会计系统能够满足会计部门的使用要求,反映最小程度的使用和维持	企业成员接受,新技术在企业工作中被采用
惯例阶段	新的管理会计系统被非会计部门和管理人员频繁用于决策与控制	企业对新技术的应用成为日常经营活动的惯例
融合阶段	新管理会计系统与现有信息系统高度集成,以支持更高层次的价值创造	新技术以整合的方式被运用以充分发挥潜能

该模型认为,变革应该是一个逐步推进的过程,如果某一阶段尚未完成,就盲目地向下一阶段冒进,很可能会招致失败。变革的各个阶段有其特定的任务和特征。企业应根据各个阶段任务的完成情况相机调整变革策略。与 Kaplan 模型相比,Cooper 模型对于企业实施管理会计变革更具有实践指导意义。

2. Anderson(1995)的修正六阶段模型

Cooper and Zmud(1990)的六阶段模型虽然描述了各阶段的变革任务,但未能指出到底是哪些因素在影响这些任务的完成。因此,Anderson(1995)借鉴信息技术实施、组织变革以及技术传播方面成熟的基本理论,以及他对美国通用汽车公司成本系统变革过程的实地研究,提出了一个修正的关于管理系统变革实施的理论框架。

该模型不仅认为变革过程是由六个连贯的阶段组成。发起阶段,变革的压力产生,它来自内部需求或外部竞争威胁,因此积极或被动地寻找解决方案。采纳阶段,选择解决方案,决定进行必要的资源投入以利于变革的实施。适用阶段,技术在组织中被开发、配置和维护,组织成员需要被培训新程序和新技术的应用。在此变革过程中,需要确定不曾预料的需求或系统缺陷。该阶段的标志是新技术的设计应用在组织成员中可以使用。接受阶段,反映组织成员对该技术最小程度的使用和维持。该阶段的标志是该技术在组织工作中被采用。惯例阶段,反映的是新系统完全取代旧的工作实践,信息技术的使用变成常规活动的一部分(有制度化的可能)。该阶段的标志是组织的治理结构被调整以适应新技术的应用,该应用成为组织成员日常经营活动的惯例。融合阶段,反映的是以一种更加全面的,并且与组织其他系统紧密相整合的方式使用新技术,不断提高组织有效性以支持更高层次的组织工作(Cooper and Zmud,1990)。该阶段的标志是在组织里新技术被运用以充分发挥潜能。

该模型的修正之处在于,每个阶段的成功实施和顺利进展到下一阶段要受到五大类背景因素的影响,即与实施相关的外部环境、个人特征、组织因素、技术因素和任务特征;并且,在实施过程的不同阶段,影响成功实施的因素不同,重要性也不同。在发起、采纳等早期阶段,企业的外部环境、任务特征、生产技术对推进变革实施有较大影响;在惯例、融合等后期阶段,新的管理会计系统对决策的支持作用以及管理者的个体特征、组织特征成为关键的影响因素。此外,变革动机、最高管理层的支持、责任的分派也是每个阶段的主要影响因素。

除了以上介绍的过程模型,还有其他研究人员对管理会计创新实践活动进行了研究。例如,Argyris and Kaplan(1994)介绍了两个过程用来实施新的管理实践活动。第一个过程是教育和倡议,变革的提倡者可以探究和阐释创新的益处,并且努力将提出的新理念转化为实际行动以获得管理层的支持。然而,这一过程也可能产生无法预料的负面效果。例如,会计人员不一定愿意接受更多的管理责任,因此抵制变革。同时,这一过程也可能揭示出以前的决策或行为一直是错误的。第二个过程,是内部承诺的产生,它要求克服来自对原有惯例的保护所造成的障碍。内部承诺的产生过程旨在促使个人实施新的理念,并付诸行动。Richards(1987)认为,变革需要长短期目标、非正式的组织拥护、良好的沟通、精确及时的成本信息、员工参与和对成本降低的奖励系统。

综上所述,过程模型的基本思想是管理会计变革要划分为逐步递进的阶段逐步实施,影响变革的关键因素以及管理变革的方法、策略要因不同的变革阶段而随机应变,也就是要根据企业内外部环境的变化而变化。

（三）管理会计变革的要素模型述评

要素模型考察了变革过程中不同要素之间如何相互结合或相互协调以促使会计变革的发生，它力求对变革基本要素分析的完备性。

1. Innes and Mitchell(1990)的三要素模型

Innes and Mitchell(1990)考虑了外部环境因素和内部因素对管理会计变革的影响。他们将影响因素分为三类，即诱发因素，如市场竞争、组织结构和生产技术变革等；催化因素，它能够直接导致管理会计的变革，如亏损严重、市场份额下降、新产品上市等；促进因素，指的是对变革必要但不充分的因素，如会计人员配备充足性、会计人员素质、母公司自治程度、信息化程度等。

该模型不足之处在于，首先，它忽略了障碍因素，即阻碍、推迟甚至阻止变革的因素，如员工对变革的态度。其次，它重在解释外在因素（例如环境）对变革的影响，但在解释变革过程如何在组织内发生，尤其是变革过程对组织成员的影响方面能力较差。变革过程只有通过人的行为才能发生，即使重要的诱发因素、催化因素和促进因素都满足，变革在没有经过相关人员的管理实施下也不会发生，也就是说这三个条件只是具备了变革的可能。

2. Cobb et al. (1995)的三要素扩展模型

Cobb et al. (1995)对 Innes and Mitchell(1990)的变革模型进行了扩展，加入了三个因素，即变革的障碍因素、变革的领导者和变革的持续推动因素。

该模型认为管理会计变革依赖于是否出现有利于变革的环境，变革的实施者是否可以根据变革情境因势利导地规划和实施变革内容，并克服变革阻力。也就是变革环境、变革实施者、变革内容这三个因素相互作用，共同影响了管理会计变革。

诱发因素、催化因素和促进因素是产生变革的必要条件，但是必须强调变革实施者在变革过程中发挥的作用。变革实施者主要是指企业高管，也包括普通员工。高管人员应根据企业特定的变革环境来规划变革方案，识别变革的阻力，并领导员工克服这些阻力。由于变革会牵扯到权力的再分配以及人员调整，因而变革的范围和深度越大，组织成员的抵制也会越大，这就需要企业高管持续不断地支持和协调各种矛盾，并积极引导变革。变革的成果应让员工共同分享，以激励他们更积极地认同和参与变革。变革内容主要是指变革方案以及需要克服的变革阻力。

Kasurinen(2002)认为，Cobb模型存在两个缺陷：一是对变革阻力的分析过于粗略，这不利于规划和执行变革；二是只强调变革的发生受制于特定变革环境，却没有意识到变革实施者的能动作用对企业的变革成功具有不可忽视的影响。

3. Kasurinen(2002)的三要素修正模型

Kasurinen(2002)进一步发展了Cobb et al.(1995)的管理会计变革模型。他们重在分析可能延缓、阻碍管理会计变革的阻力因素，将阻力因素进一步划分为三种类型：一是可能导致变革失败的"认识不清因素"，如对项目前景不确定或观点不同、僵化的权力结构等；二是扰乱变革的正常进程，甚至使之偏离预期方向的"干扰因素"，如与现有的报告系统或组织文化不同、培训不足、员工缺乏对变革的组织承诺；三是不会影响预期目标实现、但会拖延变革实施时间的"延迟因素"，如信息系统缺失或战略不清晰、资源投入不足等。

该模型的特点如下：首先，强调企业高管应首先着力解决"认识不清"方面的问题，并尽量降低干扰性阻力的影响，当然还应避免延迟性阻力的出现。这些都为企业应如何规划和执行变革、应将各种核心资源投向何处提供了重要参考。其次，企业管理会计变革的发生及其成功实施不仅是特定变革环境的产物，同时也深受变革实施者的影响。比如，高管人员的领导力、执行力越强，变革的潜能就越有可能充分释放以冲破各种变革阻力；员工对组织的依赖感和忠诚度越高，变革的推行也就越加顺利。因此，该模型强调变革主体只有努力提高自身的管理能力尤其是克服变革阻力的能力，变革才可能取得成功。

该修正模型提供了一种潜在有用的方式，可以用来分析在项目实施早期组织变革所处的环境，进而可以分析影响变革的因素，使组织在实践中尽力回避那些阻碍变革的因素。

综上所述，要素模型的理论依据主要是系统理论，因为管理会计系统实质上是一个人造系统，只有注重系统分析和系统管理，才可能促使变革取得成功。与过程模型相比，要素模型的最大特点在于，它指明变革是一个由若干要素在相互联系、相互影响过程中形成的动态有机整体，并提供了关于变革基本要素的结构化分析框架。但是，这类模型的不足在于主要是将影响变革的各类因素进行归类，没有清晰的管理会计变革成功的衡量标准，缺乏对变革过程本质的了解。

四、总结与展望

(一) 相关研究的不足之处

通过对管理会计变革与创新的理论和模型的详细回顾与评述,作者认为,国外研究从不同的研究层次和角度对管理会计变革与创新进行了考察,各有所长。但是,现有的研究也存在以下不足之处:

1. 理论模型需要进一步完善

路径模型中,Burns and Scapens(2000)的管理会计变革概念化框架提供了一个考察组织层次管理会计变革路径的通用模型(Soin et al.,2002)。该模型的主要思想是,管理会计变革的核心问题在于能否实现"制度化",即将变革目标由新的书面规则演化为企业持续、有效运用的新知识和新技能,进而成为所有成员共同认可的决策与控制的惯例模式。该模型的目的是描述和解释分析性的概念,例如可被用于解释管理会计变革的案例研究,也有助于关注变革过程的基本特征。并且,为了了解制度化过程在不同时期的特征,以及管理会计规则和惯例被复制的持续积累的过程本质,需要长期考察个体组织内的管理会计变革过程。只有这样,才有可能加深我们对管理会计系统变革的理解,并更好地预测在管理会计系统变化中遇到的问题和困难。

但是,这两位作者认为,"规则"、"惯例"和"制度"是一种分析性概念,并不能作为实证变量用一些客观方法来计量,也不能进行实证观察(Burns and Scapens,2000)。在该模型中,仅仅"行为"是可以观察的。除了"行为",其他概念越来越抽象,甚至"规则"也很难实证观察到。因此,他们认为该模型只是将管理会计变革作为一个过程进行考察的起点,并不能用于实证研究和假说检验。

过程模型中,Anderson(1995)的"阶段—因素"六阶段模型的理论基础是信息技术实施、组织变革、创新技术传播方面的理论,也包含了行为网络理论的思想。该模型对组织成本管理会计系统变革的实施过程进行了概括;其基本思想是变革的每个阶段的任务、影响变革的关键因素以及管理变革的方法、策略要因不同的变革阶段而做出相应的调整,这在本质上属于权变理论范畴(于富生等,2008)。该过程模型尤其适合解释管理会计创新的采纳引起的变革过程。

这类模型虽然强调变革必须与外部环境、制度因素、组织背景等相适应,但它对不同变革阶段影响因素的关键变量识别较为零散，缺乏一个综合性的系统分析框架，以至于其他研究者在利用过程模型进行实证检验时常得出相互矛盾的结论（Gerdin and Greve，2004）。

要素模型重在全面分析变革的基本要素，强调各要素之间的相互关系和相互协调，只有注重系统分析和系统管理，才可能促使变革取得成功。与过程模型相比，要素模型的最大特点在于，它指明了变革是一个由若干要素在相互联系、相互影响过程中形成的动态有机整体，提供了关于变革基本要素的结构化分析框架，对于设计和实施管理会计变革具有重要意义（于富生等，2008）。

2. 国内研究相对滞后

我国实务界虽然有很多企业尝试将平衡计分卡、作业成本法、全面预算管理等先进的方法运用于内部管理中，却并没有得到广泛应用（胡玉明，2008；熊焰韧、苏文兵，2008），实施率比较低，成功实施的比率更低。管理人员虽然了解这些方法，却因在推行时或在实施过程中遇到阻力和困难而放弃这些新的管理会计技术。对于这些西方先进的管理会计创新，我国学术界多是介绍和探讨其理论与实践意义，对于管理会计变革与创新这一主题基本上处于理论模型的引入阶段。对于管理会计创新在企业的实施过程、遇到的问题、影响顺利实施的因素等重要问题更是缺乏深入全面的研究。

仅有的几篇文献考察了在我国这样的重要发展中国家，国有企业如何采纳西方先进的管理会计创新，以及影响企业管理会计变革本质的因素等。这类文章阐明了管理会计创新的传播过程，有助于我们理解中国国有企业管理会计变革的本质（O'Connor et al.，2004，2006；Liu and Pan，2007；Li and Tang，2009）。例如，Li and Tang（2009）采用行动研究方法考察了一家中国国有企业设计业绩计量系统的过程。研究发现，政治约束和关键业务数据的无法获取是变革的主要障碍，然而使用者参与和现有的实践活动都有助于减缓抵制，并促使变革不断地完善。并且，中国文化的积极影响导致了一种不断进化的变革模式。Liu and Pan（2007）考察了我国国有企业组织背景下 ABC 是否能够成功实施，以及 ABC 信息是否能够有效地支持中国企业的管理决策制定。结果表明，像新兴经济体国家的其他组织一样，案例企业管理会计创新的生存和发展充满了考验和磨难。

（二）未来研究方向

基于以上分析，展望未来，我国管理会计变革与创新的研究可从以下方面进行：

第一，可借鉴已有理论、模型，在修正完善的基础上提出适合我国企业制度背景的管理会计变革与创新模型。管理会计变革与创新的各种理论和模型从不同的视角和分析层次关注不同的研究问题，已有研究并没有对这些模型进行系统的整合，形成清晰的可供借鉴的研究框架，这或许可以解释为什么这类研究的数量及受到的关注越来越少。

第二，根据修正完善的理论模型，需要深入考察企业管理会计变革与创新的一系列问题。例如，需要深入了解组织的现有规则、惯例和制度；分析变革过程中潜在的冲突和挑战；考察变革的进程、范围、程度、影响因素等过程本质，比如是否能够持续不断地影响组织中其他部门和成员的思想和行为。另外，需要考察其实施效果，例如财务业绩的提升，管理理念的改变，对组织影响的方式等等。

第三，研究方法上，管理会计变革与创新更适合采用案例、实地研究方法。Hopwood(1983)和 Kaplan(1983,1984)认为，管理会计要发现真正有价值的命题不能仅通过大样本的“远距离观察”。实地研究有利于研究人员深入组织内部获得组织运作和过程的第一手资料和原始的研究数据(Shields,1997)。李志文(2003)认为，中国的经济环境与西方多年来大量的研究成果所依存的环境不同，因此，西方多年积累下来的研究成果通常不适用于中国。

因此，我们需要进行仔细深入的实地研究，以弥补大样本实证研究的缺陷。这类研究可以打开我国企业管理会计变革过程的“黑箱”，对管理会计创新在中国企业的传播和顺利实施提供经验借鉴，使研究人员和经理人员能够更好地预测变革过程中遇到的问题和困难。只有这样，才能为我国企业引进和实施管理会计变革与创新提供极其重要和宝贵的经验证据。

参考文献

[1] 高静美、郭劲光、李宇，2010，组织变革研究体系的嬗变与中国维度的本土考量，《管理世界》，第9期，第150—164页。

[2] 高静美、李宇，2010，组织变革与发展：对未来研究的挑战，《管理世界》，第11期，第154—165页。

[3] 胡玉明、叶志锋、范海峰，2008，中国管理会计理论与实践：1978年至2008年，《会计研究》，第9期，第3—9页。

[4] 李志文，2003，浅谈实地研究：三论中国会计研究，《中国会计评论》，第1期，第241—250页。

[5] 李作战，2007，组织变革理论研究与评述，《现代管理科学》，第4期，第49—50页。

[6] 熊焰韧、苏文兵，2008，战略成本管理在中国企业有用武之地吗？《山西财经大学学报》，第10期，第112—118页。

[7] 熊焰韧、苏文兵，2008，管理会计实践发展现状与展望，《会计研究》，第11期，第84—90页。

[8] 于富生、张林，2008，企业管理会计变革理论模型研究综述，《山西财经大学学报》，第11卷第3期，第19—24页。

[9] Abernethy, M. and Chua, W., 1996, A field study of control system "redesign": The impact of institutional processes on strategic choice, *Contemporary Accounting Research*, Vol. 13, pp. 569—606.

[10] Abrahamson, E., 1991, Managerial fads and fashions: The diffusion and rejection of innovations, *Academy of Management Review*, Vol. 16, pp. 586—612.

[11] Anderson, S. W., 1995, Measuring the impact of product mix heterogeneity on manufacturing overhead cost, *The Accounting Review*, Vol. 70, pp. 363—387.

[12] Argyris, C. and Kaplan, R. S., 1994, Implementing new knowledge: The case of activity-based costing, *Accounting Horizons*, Vol. 8, pp. 83—105.

[13] Armstrong, P., 2002, The costs of activity-based management, *Accounting, Organizations and Society*, Vol. 27(1/2), pp. 99—120.

[14] Barley, S. R. and Tolbert, P. S., 1997, Institutionalization and structuration: Studying the links between action and institution, *Organization Studies*, Vol. 18, No. 1, pp. 93—117.

[15] Beck, N., Derl, J. B. and Woywode, M., 2008, Momentum or deceleration? Theoretical and methodological reflections on the analysis of organizational change, *The Academy of Management Journal*, Vol. 51, pp. 413—435.

[16] Bhimani, A., 2003, A study of the emergency of management accounting system ethos and its influence on perceived system success, *Accounting, Organization and Society*, Vol. 28, pp. 523—548.

[17] Boland, R., 1996, Why shared meanings have no place in structuration theory: A reply to Scapens and Macintosh, *Accounting, Organizations and Society*, Vol. 21, pp. 691—824.

[18] Bostrom, R. P. and Heinen, J. S., 1977, MIS problems and failures: A socio-technical perspective, *MIS Quarterly*, September, pp. 11—28.

[19] Briers, M. and Chua, W. F., 2001, The role of actor-networks and boundary objects in management accounting change: A field study of an implementation of activity-based costing, *Accounting, Organizations and Society*, Vol. 26, No. 3, pp. 237—269.

[20] Buchanan, D., Fitzgerald, L., Ketley, D., Gollop, R., Jones, J. L., Lomont, S. S., Neath, A. and Whitby, E., 2005, No going back: A review of the literature on sustaining organizational change, *International Journal of Management Review*, Vol. 7, pp. 189—205.

[21] Burns, J. and Vaivio, J., 2001, Management accounting change, *Management Accounting Research*, Vol. 12, pp. 389—402.

[22] Burns, J. and Scapens, R. W. ,2000, Conceptualizing management accounting change: An institutional framework,*Management Accounting Research* , Vol. 11, pp. 3—25.

[23] Callon, M. ,1986,Some elements of a sociology of translation,in Law, J. (Ed.), *Power, Action and Belief*, RKP, London.

[24] Carmona, S. and Gutierrez, I. ,2003, *Vogues in Management Accounting Research* , Scandinavian.

[25] Carruthers, B. G. ,1995,Accounting, ambiguity, and the new institutionalism, *Accounting, Organizations and Society*, Vol. 20, pp. 313—328.

[26] Chua, W. , 1995,Experts, networks and inscriptions in the fabrication of accounting images: A story of the representation of three public hospitals, *Accounting, Organizations and Society*, Vol. 20, pp. 111—146.

[27] Clegg, S. R. ,1989,*Frameworks of Power*, Sage Publications, London.

[28] Cobb, I. , Helliar, C. and Innes, J. ,1995, Management accounting change in a bank,*Management Accounting Research* , Vol. 6, pp. 155—175.

[29] Collier, P. ,2001, The power of accounting: A field study of local financial management in a police force,*Management Accounting Research* , Vol. 12, pp. 465—486.

[30] Cooper, R. B. and Zmud, R. W. ,1990,Information technology implementation research: A technological diffusion approach,*Management Science*, Vol. 36, pp. 123—139.

[31] Covaleski, M. A. et al. , 2003, Changes in the institutional environment and the inistitutions of governance: Extending the contributions of transaction cost economics within the management control literature,*Accounting, Organizations and Society*, Vol. 28,No. 5, pp. 45—47.

[32] Covaleski, M. , Dirsmith, M. and Samuels, S. , 1996, Management accounting research: The contributions of organizational and sociological theories,*Journal of Management Accounting Research* , Vol. 8, pp. 1—35.

[33] Covaleski, M. A. , Dirsmith, M. W. and Michelman, J. E. , 1993, An institutional theory perspective on the DRG framework, case-mix accounting systems and health-care organizations, *Accounting, Organizations and Society*, Vol. 18, pp. 65—80.

[34] Covaleski, M. A. and Dirsmith, M. W. ,1988, The use of budgetary symbols in the political arena: An historically informed field study, *Accounting, Organizations and Society*, Vol. 13, pp. 1—24.

[35] Dale, B. , Boaden, R. J. , Wilcox, M. and McQuater, R. E. ,1997,Sustaining total quality management: What are the key issues? *The TQM Magazine*, Vol. 9, pp. 372—380.

[36] Dambrin, C. , Lambert, C. and Sponem, S. ,2007,Control and change-analysing the process of institutionalization,*Management Accounting Research* , Vol. 18, pp. 172—208.

[37] Dent, J. F. ,1991, Accounting and organizational cultures: A field study of the emergence of a new organizational reality, *Account Organ, Soc*,Vol. 6, pp. 705—732.

[38] Dillard, J. F., Rigsby, J. T. and Goodman, C., 2004, The making and remaking of organization context duality and the institutionalization process, *Accounting, Auditing and Accountability Journal*, Vol. 17, No. 4, pp. 506—542.

[39] DiMaggio, P. J., 1988, Interest and agency in institutional theory, in L. Zucker (Ed.), *Institutional Patterns and Organizations: Culture and Environment*, Cambridge, MA: Ballinger, pp. 3—21.

[40] DiMaggio, P. J. and Powell, W. W., 1983, The iron cage revisited: Institutional isomorphism and collective rationality in organizational fields, *American Sociological Review*, Vol. 48, pp. 146—160.

[41] DiMaggio, P. J. and Powell, W. W., 1991, *The New Institutionalism in Organizational Analysis*, University of Chicago Press.

[42] Ezzamel, M. and Bourn, M., 1990, The roles of accounting information systems in an organization experiencing financial crisis, *Accounting, Organizations and Society*, Vol. 15, pp. 399—424.

[43] Gerdin, J. and Greve, J., 2004, Forms of contingency fit in management accounting research: A critical view, *Accounting, Organization and Society*, Vol. 29(3—4), pp. 303—326.

[44] Giddens, A., 1984, *The Constitution of Society: Outline of the Theory of Structuration*, University of California Press, Berkeley, CA.

[45] Granlund, M., 2001, Towards explaining stability in and around management accounting systems, *Manag, Account, Res*, Vol. 12, pp. 141—166.

[46] Granlund, M. and Lukka, K., 1998, It's a small world of management accounting practices, *Journal of Management Accounting Research*, Vol. 10, pp. 153—179.

[47] Greenwood, R. et al., 2002, Theorizing change: The role of professional associations in the transformation of institutionalized fields, *Academy of Management Journal*, Vol. 45, No. 1, pp. 58—80.

[48] Greenwood, R. and Hinings, C. R., 1996, Understanding radical organizational change: Bringing together the old and the new institutionalism, *Academy of Management Review*, Vol. 21, pp. 1022—1054.

[49] Hamilton, W. H., 1932, Institution, in Seligman, E. R. A. and Johnson, A. (eds), *Encyclopaedia of Social Science*, Vol. 7, No. 4, pp. 560—595.

[50] Hasselbladh, H. and Kallinikos, J., 2000, The project of rationalization: A critique and reappraisal of neo-institutionalism in organization studies, *Organization Studies*, Vol. 21, No. 4, pp. 697—720.

[51] Hopper, T. and Major, M., 2007, Extending institutional analysis through theoretical triangulation: Regulation and activity-based costing in portuguese telecommunications, *European Accounting Review*, Vol. 16, pp. 59—97.

[52] Hopwood, A. G. ,1987,The archaeology of accounting systems, *Accounting, Organizations and Society*, Vol. 12,No. 3,pp. 207—234.

[53] Hopwood,A. G. ,1983,On trying to study accounting in the contexts in which it operates,*Accounting, Organizations and Society*, Vol. 8(2/3), pp. 287—305.

[54] Innes, J. et al. ,2000, Activity-based costing in the UK's largest companies: A companies of 1994 and 1999 survey results,*Management Accounting Research* , Vol. 11,No. 3, pp. 349—362.

[55] Innes, J. and Mitchell, F. , 1990,The process of change in management accounting: Some field study evidence,*Management Accounting Research* , Vol. 1, pp. 3—19.

[56] Jones, C. T. and Dugdale, D. , 2002,The ABC bandwagon and the juggernaut of modernity, *Accounting, Organizations and Society*, Vol. 27, pp. 121—163.

[57] Kanter, R. , Stein, B. and Jick, T. ,1992, *The Challenge of Organizational Change: How Companies Experience it and Leaders Guide It*, New York: Free Press.

[58] Kaplan, R. S. , 1983, Measuring, manufacturing performance: A new challenge for managerial accounting research,*The Accounting Review*, Vol. 58, No. 4,October, pp. 686—705.

[59] Kaplan,R. S. ,1984,The evolution of management accounting, *The Accounting Review*, Vol. 59, No. 3, July, pp. 390—418.

[60] Kasurinen, T. ,2002,Exploring management accounting change: The case of balanced scorecard implementation,*Management Accounting Research* , Vol. 13, pp. 323—343.

[61] Kwon, T. H. and Zmud, R. W. ,1987,Unifying the fragmented models of information systems implementation, In R. J. Boland and R. Hirscheim (Eds), *Critical Issues in Information Systems Research* , New York, NY: Wiley, pp. 227—251.

[62] Latour, B. ,1987,*Science in Action: How to Follow Scientists and Engineers through Society*, Open University Press, Milton Keyness.

[63] Lewin, K. ,1952, Group decision and social change, *Readings in Social Psychology*, edited by T. M. Newcomb and E. L. Hartley,New York:Henry Holt and Co.

[64] Li, P. and Tang, G. L. , 2009,Performance measurement design within its organisational context-Evidence from China, *Management Accounting Research* , Vol. 20, pp. 193—207.

[65] Libby, T. and Waterhouse, J. H. ,1996,Predicting change in management accounting systems, *Journal of Management Accounting Research* ,Vol. 8, pp. 137—150.

[66] Liu, L. Y. J. and Pan, F. ,2007,The implementation of activity-based costing in China: An innovation action research approach, *British Accounting Review*, Vol. 39, pp. 249—264.

[67] Lukka, K. , 2007,Management accounting change and stability:Loosely coupled rules and routines in action, *Management Accounting Research* , Vol. 18, pp. 76—101.

[68] Malmi, T. ,1999, Activity-based costing diffusion across organizations: An exploratory empirical analysis of finish firms,*Accounting, Organizations and Society*, Vol. 24, pp. 649—672.

[69] Martinez, R. J. ,1999,Efficiency motives and normative forces: Combining transaction costs and institutional logic,*Journal of Management*, Vol. 26, pp. 27—43.

[70] Meyer, J. ,1994,Rationalized environments, in W. R. Scott and J. Meyer (Eds), *Institutionalized Environments*, Sage Publications,pp. 28—54.

[71] Meyer, J. W. and Rowan, B. ,1977,Institutionalised organisations: Formal structures as myth and ceremony,*American Journal of Sociology*, Vol. 83, No. 2,pp. 340—363.

[72] Miller, P. ,1991,Accounting innovation beyond the enterprise: Problematizing investment decisions and programming economic growth in the UK in the 1960s,*Accounting, Organizations and Society*, Vol. 16, pp. 733—762.

[73] Moll, J. and Hoque, Z. ,2011,Budgeting for legitimacy: The case of an Australian University, *Accounting, Organization and Society*, Vol. 36, pp. 86—101.

[74] Monteiro, R. D. C. and Zanjacomo, P. R. ,2000,General interior-point maps and existence of weighted paths for nonlinear semidefinite complementarity problems,*Mathematics of Operations Research*, Vol. 25, No. 3, pp. 381—399.

[75] Mouritsen, J. , 1994, Rationality, institutions and decision making: Reflections on march and olsen's rediscovering institutions,*Accounting, Organizations and Society*, Vol. 19, No. 2, pp. 193—211.

[76] N. , R. S. ,1990, The four-stage model of cost system design, *Management Accounting*, February, pp. 22—26.

[77] Nelson, R. R. and Winter, S. G. ,1982,*An Evolutionary Theory of Economic Change*,Boston: Harvard University Press.

[78] O'Connor, N. G. , Chow, C. W. and Wu, A. ,2004, The adoption of Western management accounting/controls in China's state-owned enterprises during economic transition,*Accounting, Organizations and Society*, Vol. 29, pp. 349—375.

[79] O'Connor, N. G. , Deng, J. and Luo, Y. ,2006, Political constraints, organization design and performance measurement in China's state-owned enterprises, *Accounting, Organization and Society*, Vol. 21, pp. 157—177.

[80] Palepu, M. ,1987, The anatomy of an accounting change, in W. J. Bruns Jr. , R. S. Kaplan (eds), *Accounting, Management-Field Study Perspectives*, Boston, MA, Harvard Business School Press.

[81] Pasmore,W. and Fagans, M. , 1992, Participation, individual development and organizational change:A review and synthesis,*Journal of Management*,Vol. 18, No. 2, pp. 375—397.

[82] Perrow, C. , 1986,*Comples Organizations: A Critical Essay*,3rd ed. , Randon House, New York, NY.

[83] Pettigrew,A. M. ,Massini,S. and Numagami,T. ,2000,Innovative forms of organizing in Europe and Japan,*European Management Journal*, Vol. 18, pp. 259—273.

[84] Piderit, S. K. , 2000, Rethinking resistance and recognizing ambivalence: A multidimensional view of attitudes toward an organization change,*The Academy of Management Review*, Vol. 25, pp. 783—794.

[85] Preston, A. M. , Copper, D. J. and Coombs, R. W. , 1992, Fabricating budgets: A study of production of management budgeting in the National Health Service, *Accounting, Organization and Society*, Vol. 17, pp. 561—593.

[86] Quattrone, P. and Hopper, T. M. ,2001,What does organisational change mean? Speculations on a taken for granted category, *Management Accounting Research*, Vol. 12, No. 4, pp. 403—436.

[87] Richardson, A. J. ,1987, Accounting as a legitimating institution,*Accounting, Organization and Society*, Vol. 12,pp. 341—355.

[88] Scapens, R. W. ,1994,Never mind the gap: Towards an institutional perspective of management accounting practices, *Management Accounting Research*, Vol. 5, pp. 301—321.

[89] Scapens, R. W. ,2006, Understanding management accounting practices: A personal journey, *Br. Account. Rev*, Vol. 38, pp. 1—30.

[90] Scott, R. W. and Meyer, J. W. , 1991,The organization of societal sectors: Propositions and early evidence,in W. W. Powell and P. J. DiMaggio (Eds.), *The New Institutionalism in Organizational Analysis*, Chicago: University of Chicago Press, pp. 108—140.

[91] Scott, W. R. ,2001,*Institutions and Organizations*, 2nd edn (Thousand Oaks, CA: Sage).

[92] Shields, M. D. ,1997, Research in management accounting by North Americans in the 1990s, *Journal of Management Accounting Research*, Vol. 9, pp. 3—61.

[93] Siti-Nabiha, A. K. and Scapens, R. W. ,2005,Stability and change: An institutionalist study of management accounting change,*Accounting, Audition & Accountability Journal*, Vol. 18, pp. 44—73.

[94] Soin,K. ,Seal,W. and Cullen, J. ,2002,ABC and organizational change: An institutional perspective,*Management Accounting Research*,Vol. 13, pp. 249—271.

[95] Veblen, T. ,1898, Why is economics not an evolutionary science? *Quarterly Journal of Economics*, Vol. 12, pp. 373—397.

[96] Veblen, T. ,1919,*The Place of Science in Modern Civilisation and Other Essays*,New York, Huebsch, pp. 56—81.

[97] Weber, M. , 1958, Science as a vocation, Daedalus, *Science and the Modern World View* (Winter), Vol. 87, No. 1, pp. 111—134.

[98] Zucker, L. G. , 1977,The role of institutionalization in cultural persistence,*American Review*, Vol. 42, No. 4, pp. 726—743.

[99] Zucker, L. G. , 1991, Markets for bureaucratic authority and control: Information quality in professions and services, *Research in the Sociology of Organizations*, Vol. 8, pp. 157—190.

A Review of the Literature on Management Accounting Change and Innovation

LIN ZHOU
(*Henan University of Economics and Law*)
FEI PAN
(*Shanghai University of Finance and Economics*)
YANJUN LIU
(*Newcastle University, UK*)

Abstract This paper reviews the existing theoretical analysis and path models, process models, element models of management accounting change and innovation, points out the scope and inadequacy of existing theory models. Then this paper provides detailed countermeasures and suggestions for future research.

Key words Management Accounting Change, Innovation, Models

上市公司高管薪酬激励的梯度效应研究

蒋　涛　刘运国*

摘　要　本文选取1998—2010年上市公司为研究样本,发现薪酬激励具有梯度效应:盈利公司的薪酬业绩敏感性随着业绩增长逐渐降低,而亏损公司的薪酬业绩敏感性随着亏损加大逐渐增加。垄断行业基本不存在梯度效应,而高科技行业梯度效应较强。本文研究结果验证了高管薪酬契约制定得越细致越能够节约代理成本。

关键词　薪酬契约,梯度效应,行业特征

一、引　言

契约是古老的人类行为调节方式。思想家卢梭指出社会契约要解决的根本问题是:"要寻找出一种结合的形式,使它能维护和保障每个参与人的人身和财富,并且在这个结合体的个人又只不过是在服从自己本人,且像以前一样自由。"上述描述归纳了契约调节人类之间的行为具有的特点,契约关系的建立是自由选择的结果,权利和义务的约束通过契约表达。契约关系是资本主义商品自由交换的基本保障。代理理论出现以后通过薪酬契约的安排来缓解代理问题成为学者追逐的热点。委托代理关系中代理人和委托人是相对独立的自由人,各自追求自身利益最大化,通过合理的契约安排,缓解双方的利益冲突,实

---

* 蒋涛(通信作者),重庆理工大学会计学院,通信地址:重庆市南岸区南兴路230号交通大厦21-4,邮编:400060,E-mail:wunutao@sina.com.cn;刘运国,中山大学管理学院/中山大学成本与管理会计研究中心,E-mail:mnsygliu@mail.sysu.edu.cn。作者感谢教育部人文社科一般项目(批准号:11YJA790094)、中央高校基本科研业务费专项资金资助项目(批准号:1109153;11nkjl04)、国家自然科学基金项目(批准号:71032006、71372150)的支持,同时感谢中国会计学会管理会计与应用专业委员会2012年度学术研讨会评论人的意见。本文选自中国会计学会管理会计分委员会2012年年会论文,文章由胡玉明教授接受。

现委托人与代理人的共赢。因此,薪酬契约能够调节委托人与代理人的行为方式,降低企业的代理成本。

Jenson and Meckling(1976)指出代理成本主要由委托人监督代理人的成本、代理人的保证成本以及剩余损失(因代理人与委托人利益存在差异而形成的代理人决策与委托人利益最大化决策之间的偏差)组成。代理人薪酬与业绩挂钩的薪酬政策有利于缓和代理人与委托人的利益冲突,降低委托人的监督成本以及代理人的保证成本。代理理论假设薪酬与业绩相关能够减少代理成本,提高企业的绩效,实证研究的结果却对薪酬与业绩敏感性产生了怀疑。这些怀疑主要体现在两个方面。首先,薪酬业绩敏感性太小。Jensen and Murphy(1999)的研究结果与理论预期不符,业绩与高管的薪酬关联度很小。股东财富增加 1 000 美元,相应高管薪酬只增加了 3.25 美元,其中底薪和奖金只增加了 0.22 美元。其次,薪酬业绩非对称性问题,即公司高管会因业绩上升而获得薪酬奖励,而在业绩下降时薪酬的降低却很少。例如,企业会在市场行情好的时候,把市场指标纳入高管的薪酬考核,却在市场行情不好的时候放弃这些指标;差的市场回报没有受到薪酬惩罚,而高的市场回报却能得到薪酬奖励;增加 CEO 薪酬对提高企业的规模和股东财富均有一定的促进作用,但降低 CEO 薪酬却不仅不能提高企业规模和股东财富,反而会对其产生一定的负面影响;业绩上升时薪酬的增加幅度显著高于业绩下降时薪酬的减少幅度(Garvey and Milbourn,2006;Shaw and Zhang,2010;刘斌等,2003;方军雄,2009)。

不管是薪酬业绩敏感性太小,还是薪酬业绩敏感的不稳健都对通过薪酬契约解决代理问题提出了质疑。如果薪酬业绩敏感性太小,通过薪酬契约解决代理问题并没有什么实际作用。同样,薪酬业绩非对称性会让委托人承担更大的损失。假设一家公司高管通过盈余管理让本期增加盈利 1 000 万元,下一期减少 1 000 万元,总的盈利本质上没有变化。如果存在薪酬非对称性,公司高管本期会因为盈利而获取薪酬奖励,但是在下一期盈利减少时不受到薪酬惩罚。这样一个简单的举动,就能让高管在没有增加利润的同时获取更多的薪酬,间接鼓励高管做导致企业会计业绩波动增大的盈余管理。

针对前面研究的质疑,是否是因为忽略薪酬契约激励的梯度效应特征所造成的。如果薪酬激励是伴随业绩变动的一个变量,既能出现忽大忽小又能出现时而敏感时而不敏感的情况,那么无论敏感性太小还是非对称性问题可能都没有想象中严重。本文以薪酬契约激励的梯度效应这种动态特征为研究对象,说明代理成本更低的契约能够更好地满足委托人期望，引导代理人的行为。

什么是薪酬激励的梯度效应？下面我们来分析两种不同形式的薪酬契约。第一种薪酬契约：完成1 000万元利润，委托人给予代理人实现利润金额2%的薪酬奖励；亏损1 000万元，按照亏损金额的2%降薪。第二种薪酬契约：完成1 000万元的利润，对0—500万元部分，予以2%的薪酬奖励；对500万—800万元部分，予以1.5%的薪酬奖励；对于800万—1 000万元部分，予以1%的薪酬奖励；超过1 000万元部分，不再给予薪酬奖励。笔者把第二种契约定义为具有梯度效应的薪酬契约。梯度效应可以分为边际递增效应或者递减效应。例如，亏损500万元，从薪酬中扣减亏损金额的5%；亏损超过500万元，对于超过500万元部分的10%从薪酬中扣除，这是边际递增的梯度效应，而前面所指的是边际递减的梯度效应。

具有梯度效应的薪酬契约更加节约代理成本。同样是完成1 000万元利润，具有梯度效应的契约委托人付出的薪酬更低，委托人用较小的代价解决代理问题，客观上降低了代理成本。读者会反驳这样的契约安排同时降低了代理人对更高业绩的追求。这种考虑非常正确，事实上企业也不是总以利润最大化为经营目标。一方面，利润最大化战略增加企业经营风险，破产风险提升；另一方面，利润最大化战略本身存在一定问题。Armen(1950)认为由于不确定性的存在，企业的产出就是一个概率分布，要想从中找出利润最大的点根本不可能，因此我们追求的仅仅是一个最优的分布而不是最大的分布。[1]因此，具有梯度效应的薪酬契约鼓励代理人以适度的业绩为追求目标，保障委托人资产安全的同时，委托人也付出更少的薪酬成本解决代理问题，客观上降低了代理成本。另外，采用具有梯度效应的薪酬契约，代理人会偏好更加“平滑”的业绩。假设本期利润很高，下一期利润很低。本期的薪酬奖励会因梯度效应打折，导致总的薪酬奖励降低。相反，如果两期利润相近，受梯度效应影响不大，总的薪酬就较高。采用第一种薪酬契约，公司高管因为业绩上升获取的薪酬奖励较多，这些高管为了获取薪酬奖励，极力追求利润，加大公司经营风险，导致企业业绩波动性变大，反过来代理人薪酬风险也加大，委托人需要支付更多的薪酬来弥补高管承受的风险，实际上加大了代理成本。

[1] 就如我们买卖股票一样，最理想的状态是最高点卖出，最低点买入股票。事实上我们永远不知道最高点和最低点在哪里。对基金经理的激励也不能以最高点卖出、最低点买入为目标。

刘洪军(2004)认为如果个别人的机会主义行为总能获得宽恕,并且在违规中获得额外收益,其他理性人就会效仿泛滥的机会主义行为,从而可能使传统的契约丧失效率,面临崩溃的危险。有了惩罚的威胁,遭到惩罚的预期也必然纳入行动者的越轨成本。Arvey et al. (1984)研究发现惩罚是提升员工工作动机、绩效、工作满意度和其他需要的态度和行为结果的有效手段。惩罚是契约的维护机制,有利于契约的执行。如果薪酬契约只规定薪酬奖励,却没有薪酬惩罚,则委托人事实上承担所有的风险,薪酬契约不但不能缓解代理问题,反而会加大代理成本。根据第一种契约,代理人损失委托人全部资产仅仅受到全部薪酬扣除的惩罚,这是任何一个委托人都不愿意接受的薪酬契约。采用第二种薪酬契约,代理人即使损失委托人少量资产,也可能受到全部薪酬扣除的惩罚。采用边际递增的薪酬惩罚契约,代理人即使不能避免亏损也会尽量减少亏损,用较小的惩罚来替代更为严重的惩罚。这种避免代理人破罐子破摔的契约,客观上也降低了代理成本。

大量的学者研究薪酬契约时都采用第一种契约,研究业绩对薪酬、业绩变化对薪酬变化、股东财富对薪酬、股东财富变化对薪酬变化的影响(Murphy, 1999)。在这些研究中求出的薪酬业绩敏感性系数均为静态的常数。本文研究发现薪酬契约存在梯度效应,薪酬业绩敏感性系数成为一个伴随业绩变动的变量。具体而言,在薪酬奖励情况下,薪酬业绩敏感性随着业绩增长而递减;而在薪酬惩罚情况下,薪酬业绩敏感性随着损失增加而递增。垄断企业梯度效应更弱,而高科技企业梯度效应更强。本文贡献如下:首先,突破以往将薪酬业绩敏感性系数当成一个常量研究其大小,指出薪酬业绩敏感性是一个变量,存在梯度效应。本文研究可以部分解释薪酬业绩敏感性较小的问题。随着业绩上升,敏感性逐渐降低,总体上减少薪酬业绩敏感性程度。[2]其次,薪酬不对称文献指出高管会因业绩增加而得到薪酬奖励,而业绩下降时薪酬的惩罚却很少。本文指出薪酬奖励也不是无止境的,会逐渐减少直至消失。而业绩下降导致委托人损失的情况下,将会受到边际递增的惩罚。非对称性文献主要指出奖励幅度大于惩罚幅度的问题,本文突破性发现存在惩罚幅度大于奖励幅度的情况。

[2] 亏损公司样本只占总样本的10%不到,并且在以往学者的研究中往往都剔除处理,不会对以往学者的薪酬业绩敏感性大小的结论产生影响。

二、理论分析与研究假设

随着公司治理水平的提高，薪酬业绩关联越来越被认可。杜兴强等(2007)研究发现，高层管理人员薪酬与公司以及股东财富前后两期的变化均呈正相关关系，证明了高管薪酬的激励作用。在薪酬业绩相关被认可的基础上，一些学者提出奖励方案中风险设置非常重要，对风险逆向的经理通过基本薪酬来限制其最低风险；同时，风险的上限也会被限制，否则高管会什么事情都去做以求牟利，因此薪酬契约也规定有封顶红利(Healy，1985；斯科特，2006；Murphy，1999)。以上研究均采用第一种契约模式，没有看到薪酬业绩敏感性的梯度特征。现实中大量公司采用具有梯度效应的薪酬契约。

上海现代制药股份有限公司高级管理人员的薪酬方案明确指出：实际利润总额完成值达到考核指标值80%以上(含80%)时，绩效奖励按以下比例分段提取：① 完成的利润总额在考核指标100%以内(含100%)部分，按调整后的合并报表利润总额的1.5%提取绩效奖励；② 完成的利润总额在考核指标100%—120%(含120%)部分，按调整后的合并报表利润总额的2%提取绩效奖励；③ 完成的利润总额超过考核指标120%以上部分，按调整后的合并报表利润总额的1%提取绩效奖励。[3]

思达高科技股份有限公司高层管理人员的薪酬方案指出：① 考核年度实际利润小于基准利润的50%(不含50%)，扣减高管人员基本工资的30%；② 考核年度实际利润大于基准利润的50%(含50%)而小于基准利润70%，扣减高管人员基本工资的20%；③ 考核年度实际利润大于基准利润的70%(含70%)而小于基准利润，扣减高管人员基本工资的10%；④ 考核年度实际利润等于基准利润，足额支付高管人员的基本年薪，但不提取奖励基金。[4]

下面笔者从理论上分析具有梯度效应薪酬契约的合理性。

首先，代理人不一定固守风险逆向偏好。以往大量学者假定代理人风险逆向。Gray and Cannella (1997)指出委托人与代理人拥有不一样的风险。一方

---

[3] 资料来源：国信证券，《现代制药(600420)高级管理人员薪酬方案》，2009年12月2日，http://www.guosen.com.cn/webd/public/infoDetail.jsp? infoid=8517805

[4] 资料来源：中证网，《思达高科：高层管理人员薪酬方案》，2010年3月16日，http://stock.cs.com.cn/stock/stocknotice.php? noticeid=57691071

面高管没有足够的财富去承担风险,另一方面如果一个人只能专注于一项投资,那么他必须风险逆向。代理人主要按劳取酬,只能服务于一家企业,无法做到人力资本的分散投资来规避风险。对于高业绩薪酬敏感的激励政策,代理人天生有转移风险的欲望。实际上代理人一直风险逆向的假定存在问题。如果追求风险获取的收益远远大于失败的损失,代理人有可能从风险逆向到风险喜好转移。Smith and Stulz(1985)认为委托人可以通过薪酬契约设计改变高管的风险偏好。薪酬与企业价值是凹函数关系时,经理人是风险规避偏好;如果是凸函数,则经理人从风险规避向追求风险转移。MacCrimmon and Donald(1986)发现随着赌注的增加参与人有更多的风险逆向。例如,参加一项赌注,赢了获得一元奖励,输了损失一元,参与人基本忽略其输赢风险,但是赌注变成一百万元时,参与者会变得风险逆向。但是如果输了损失一元,赢了获得一百万元时,参与者会变得风险喜好。该文作者同时指出高职位经理比低职位经理有更多的风险偏好,这也说明了控制代理人风险的重要性。以上研究均说明代理人不一定是一直风险逆向偏好,控制高级经理人的风险偏好也是薪酬契约必须考虑的因素之一。

其次,代理人的理赔能力有限,必须控制其风险偏好水平。委托代理关系中委托人与代理人财产数量严重不对称,相对于巨额的委托人财产,代理人没有相应的资产作为理赔担保。经营造成的委托人的损失,代理人无法全额赔偿,代理人的损失远远小于委托人。过度追求业绩能给代理人带来可观的回报的同时却因为自身财富远远小于委托人而不用承担对等的风险。因此,委托人必须要控制代理人的风险。采用第一种薪酬契约安排,代理人会因为业绩的上升一直获取薪酬奖励,可能造就代理人以小博大过度追求业绩的行为。成功了代理人可以获取大量薪酬奖励,失败了自身财富有限没法全额赔付委托人损失,收益与风险的不对等容易导致代理人由谨慎经营向偏好风险转变。代理人偏好风险容易导致委托人资产损失,这种契约安排满足委托人资产保值增值的需要却忽略了资产安全的需要,并不符合委托人多目标的需求。另一方面,代理人也并不是被动接受薪酬契约,而是根据自身风险承受能力调整契约行为,这是一个双方博弈的过程。Randolph and Edward(1994)研究发现企业风险越大,高管拥有更少的期权等风险性薪酬,说明代理人也不愿意承受过多风险。一旦委托人要求代理人承受过多的风险,代理人反过来会要求更高的薪酬,委托人需要付出更高的薪酬成本。

最后，具有梯度效应的薪酬契约能够较好地控制代理人的风险偏好，降低代理成本。设想一家企业有两种业绩组合：第一种，业绩好的时候能够盈利900万元，差的时候盈利100万元；第二种，业绩好的时候能够盈利600万元，差的时候盈利400万元，两种状况发生的可能性均为50%。这两种业绩组合的数学期望一样都为500万元，但是业绩组合一的方差远远大于业绩组合二。同时有两种薪酬契约可供选择。采用第一种薪酬契约，给予代理人2%的薪酬奖励；采用第二种具有梯度效应的薪酬契约，500万元以下盈利给予2%的薪酬奖励，500万元以上盈利给予代理人1%的薪酬奖励。[5]代理人获得的薪酬奖励见表1。通过表1，可以发现采用第一种薪酬契约，无论是业绩组合一还是业绩组合二，代理人获得的薪酬奖励没有差异。采用第二种薪酬契约，无论是业绩组合一还是业绩组合二，代理人获得的薪酬奖励均小于采用第一种薪酬契约，同时业绩组合二发生时代理人获得的薪酬奖励大于业绩组合一。从中可以推断，采用带有梯度效应的薪酬契约，代理人更愿意选择风险小的经营策略。在相同回报（数学期望）条件下，具有梯度效应的薪酬契约比第一种契约付出的薪酬成本更小，因此代理成本更低；其次采用具有梯度效应的薪酬契约在回报相同的情况下，代理人会选择风险（方差）较低的策略。[6]同理，出现亏损时，采用边际递增的薪酬惩罚，代理人受到的薪酬惩罚更大。相同亏损情况下，方差更大的亏损组合受到的薪酬惩罚更高。

表1　薪酬奖励差异

第一种薪酬契约				第二种薪酬契约			
业绩组合一		业绩组合二		业绩组合一		业绩组合二	
情况一	情况二	情况一	情况二	情况一	情况二	情况一	情况二
900万元	100万元	600万元	400万元	900万元	100万元	600万元	400万元
薪酬奖励				薪酬奖励			
10万元		10万元		8万元		9.5万元	

为什么薪酬奖励采用的是边际递减的契约，而薪酬惩罚采用的是边际递增

[5] 这里把业绩的数学期望500万元作为梯度标准，如果采用其他标准，结果会有所变化，但是无论怎样代理人获得的薪酬奖励均小于采用第一种契约。

[6] 尽管代理人选择业绩组合一，委托人付出的薪酬更低，但是委托人为了降低风险，还是愿意诱导代理人朝业绩组合二努力，不管怎样采用具有梯度效应的契约委托人付出的薪酬小于第一种契约。当然如果梯度标准不是500万元，采用业绩组合一获得的薪酬奖励也可能高于业绩组合二，此时代理人可能选择相同回报情况下风险较大的策略，所以梯度标准的选择也很重要。

的契约？笔者认为对于薪酬奖励，代理人不用提供担保，委托人需要控制的是代理人过度追求风险的倾向，因此采用边际递减的激励契约；而对于薪酬惩罚，代理人能够提供的最大信用担保就是基本工资，代理人的基本工资明显与委托人的巨量财富不对称，在对赌协议中双方获取同样比例的损失明显对委托人不公，因此采用边际递增的惩罚。

从前面的论述可以看出，具有梯度效用的薪酬契约能够更好地引导代理人对风险的控制，降低代理成本。根据以上分析笔者提出假设1：

假设1 薪酬契约具有梯度效应。具体而言，在实现盈利情况下，高管获得的薪酬奖励随着业绩的增加而边际递减；在亏损情况下，高管获得的薪酬惩罚随着亏损程度的加大而边际递增。

Mark and Banker(2000)研究发现企业在选择薪酬激励方式时会充分考虑自身行业的特点。一般认为，IT行业面临更多的市场风险，更需要长期激励高管，因此IT行业更喜欢采用期权激励高管。然而该文作者认为如果控制住这些行业特殊的经济因素，IT行业的期权激励与其他行业相比没有差异。Joskow et al.(1996)通过对86家电力企业进行调查，发现这些公司高管的薪酬因政府管制的存在而更低。因此，行业差异的存在，导致薪酬契约在解决代理问题时也会存在差异。与其他行业相比，垄断行业不需要太多的薪酬激励来解决代理问题：很难分清垄断行业公司业绩的实现是靠垄断之手取得，还是靠代理人的辛苦工作取得，因此依据业绩来奖励代理人不成立。Aggarwal and Samwick (1999)研究发现由于垄断企业商品价格坚挺，股东不需要通过薪酬契约去激励高管打价格战，因此在薪酬契约中很少采用相对业绩评价。

另一方面，垄断企业的职能与普通企业也不一致，很多垄断企业还肩负着社会公共服务的职能。比如，能源企业价格受管制，国际航空公司还要承担国际救援等任务。如果这些企业不是完全利润导向，用薪酬奖励来激励代理人取得更好的业绩也就不完全成立。如果垄断行业的高管薪酬与业绩过度挂钩，则会诱导高管产生提价动力，垄断企业获取利润的最好办法就是提价。例如，上市公司中国石油、中国石化处于特许经营地位，同时面临价格管制。如果他们的利润不能得到保障，这类企业就会通过涨价来确保利润，如果政府拒绝他们的涨价要求，市场就会面临供给不足的危险，大量的汽车加不到燃油。因此，抑制这类企业的涨价冲动也是薪酬契约必须要考虑的内容。所以这类公司的薪酬业绩敏感性不能太高。如果不存在薪酬业绩敏感性，自然也就不存在梯度效应。

高科技行业的技术特征注定委托人与代理人之间存在更多的信息不对称，委托人监督代理人存在更多的困难，需要更多的薪酬激励来解决代理问题。Xue(2007)指出高管薪酬与企业的战略有关。如果公司采用以会计信息为衡量标准的薪酬契约，高管为了规避自己研发的高风险，则偏好采用购买技术的策略；相反，以权益薪酬为主的高管喜欢采用自己研发技术的策略，说明薪酬契约可以影响企业的研发行为。根据太和顾问2010薪酬调查报告发现，高科技行业企业对于一般员工和主管级员工的薪酬给付主要以吸引和保留为主，基本月薪和福利占据薪酬的主要部分，促使员工感到薪酬的稳定性和企业的归属感，保证大多数员工能够安心工作。经理层和总监层岗位的薪酬结构中，高科技企业大多注重绩效薪酬占比，变动收入能够起到很好的激励作用，这样的契约安排能够在合理地控制薪酬成本的同时调动中高层管理人员的工作积极性。[7]这说明高科技企业委托人与代理人信息更加不对称，需要用薪酬来激励高管，因此高科技行业的薪酬业绩敏感性系数较高。同时，与其他行业相比，高科技行业经营风险更大，过度追求利润，容易增加破产风险，因此高科技行业不宜一直采用强的激励薪酬策略，需要在激励代理人的同时，加入梯度效应，控制激励程度，代理人既追求业绩，又不过度追求业绩，同时满足委托人资产保值增值与资产安全的需要。根据以上分析提出假设2：

假设2a　与其他行业相比，垄断企业的薪酬业绩敏感性系数降低，梯度效应也较弱；

假设2b　与其他行业相比，高科技企业薪酬业绩敏感性系数较高，梯度效应也较高。

三、研究设计与样本选择

（一）研究设计

根据前面的理论分析，设计二次方程模型验证薪酬业绩敏感性具有梯度效应。完整回归模型如下：

---

[7] 资料来源：《薪酬，如何不"心愁"？—太和顾问2010薪酬调查报告解析》，Human Resource Management，2011/03

$$\text{Comp} = \alpha + \beta_1 \text{performance} + \beta_2 \text{performance}^2 + \text{Control variable} + \text{indus} + \text{years} + \varepsilon \quad (1)$$

其中，因变量 Comp 表示薪酬金额最高的前三名高级管理人员的报酬总额除以3取对数，自变量 performance 用净利润作为业绩的替代变量。上市公司大量采用净利润作为薪酬的考核指标。例如，上市公司江苏中联电气股份有限公司的高管薪酬管理办法：高管考核采用百分制计分，① 利润总额(40 分)；② 销售总量(20 分)；③ 生产总量(20 分)，利润指标占考核标准的 40%。上海现代制药股份有限公司的高管薪酬管理办法将营业总收入、利润总额、净资产收益率作为主要考核指标。[8]基于以上考虑，本文选用净利润作为业绩的替代变量。Lambert(2001)指出采用相对业绩评价能剔除代理人所受共同市场噪音的影响，委托人仅仅使用了代理人业绩中“特质的”组成部分来评估代理人。为了增强文章的稳健性，引入经过行业、年度中位数调整的相对净利润作为业绩的替代变量。根据利润的完成情况，笔者将总样本分成两组：净利润大于 0 组，代理人应该获得薪酬奖励；净利润小于 0 组(即亏损组)，代理人应该受到薪酬惩罚。控制变量 Control variable 采用方军雄(2009)的做法，将营业收入的对数、资产负债率、是否是国企、第一大股东持股比例、是否是西部企业、是否是东部企业、是否同时发行 B 股、是否两职合一、独董比例、是否存在薪酬考核委员会，以及行业和年度控制变量。为防止异常值影响，所有变量在 1%winsorize。

对模型(1)求一阶偏导得：dcomp/dperformance $= \beta_1 + 2\beta_2$ performance，薪酬业绩敏感性系数为 dcomp/dperformance。其中，β_1 为常量，$\beta_2$performance 为一个变量，薪酬业绩敏感性系数为一个变量，主要由 β_2 决定。根据假设 1，预计 β_1 为正，随着盈利增加，薪酬增加；β_2 为负，随着盈利的增加，$\beta_2$performance 变大，$\beta_1 + 2\beta_2$performance 变小。高管获得的薪酬奖励随着业绩的增加边际递减。在亏损情况下，预计 β_1 为正，随着亏损的增加薪酬降低，β_2 为负，随着亏损的增加，$\beta_2$performance 变大，$\beta_1 + 2\beta_2$performance 变大。亏损情况下，高管获得的薪酬奖励随着亏损的增加边际递增。

其次，只考虑业绩大于 0 的样本。生成回归模型如下：

---

[8] 资料来源：广发网，《中联电气(002323)高管人员绩效考核和薪酬管理办法》，2011 年 4 月 19 日，http://www.gf.com.cn/commons/infoList.jsp? docId = 826670；资料来源：国信证券，《现代制药(600420)高级管理人员薪酬方案》，2009 年 12 月 02 日，http://www.guosen.com.cn/webd/public/infoDetail.jsp? infoid=8517805；方军雄(2009)也将净利润作为业绩的替代变量。

$$\begin{aligned}\text{Comp} = & \alpha + \beta_1 \text{performance} + \beta_2 \text{performance}^2 \\ & + \beta_3 D + \beta_4 D \times \text{performance} + \beta_5 D \times \text{performance}^2 \\ & + \text{Control variable} + \text{indus} + \text{years} + \varepsilon \end{aligned} \tag{2}$$

其中，D 表示行业特征，是否是垄断企业或者高科技企业，通过模型(2)，检验不同行业特征薪酬激励的梯度效应的差异。根据假设 2：与其他行业相比，高科技企业薪酬业绩敏感性系数较高，梯度效应也较高。在 $\beta_1>0$ 及 $\beta_2<0$ 的情况下，如果交乘项 $\beta_4>0$，$\beta_1+\beta_4$ 两个系数符号相同都为正，表明激励业绩敏感性系数更高；如果交乘项 $\beta_5<0$，梯度效应等于 $\beta_2+\beta_5$，两个系数符号相同都为负，表明梯度效应也更强。同样根据假设 2：与其他行业相比，垄断企业的薪酬业绩敏感性系数较低、梯度效应也较弱。$\beta_4<0$，$\beta_5>0$，表明两者更弱。

（二）数据来源与描述性统计

样本来源于 CCER 色诺芬金融研究数据库以及国泰安数据库，考虑公司治理数据库最早出现于 1998 年，选用 1998—2010 年全部 A 股上市公司样本，剔除金融行业公司样本以及数据缺失公司样本，得到样本 12 816 个。样本情况见表 2。

表 2　研究变量描述性统计结果

变量	样本数	均值	标准差	最小值	最大值
高管薪酬	12 816	236 193.9	318 416.5	2 000	6 800 000
国企	12 816	0.650	0.476	0	1
第一大股东持股比例	12 816	0.393	0.165	0.084	0.770
西部	12 816	0.159	0.366	0	1
东部	12 816	0.488	0.499	0	1
B 股	12 816	0.069	0.253	0	1
两职合一	12 816	0.151	0.358	0	1
独董比例	12 816	0.491	0.205	0.2	0.8
薪酬考核委员会	12 816	0.647	0.477	0	1
营业收入	12 816	3.738	32.772	0	1 465.415
资产负债率	12 816	0.479	0.192	0.064	0.915
净利润(盈利样本)	11 459	0.257	2.644	0	139.871
净利润(亏损样本)	1 357	−0.196	0.515	−9.149	−0.001
中位数调整后净利润(盈利样本)	11 459	0.106	0.335	−0.465	2.317
中位数调整后净利润(亏损样本)	1 357	−0.173	0.125	−0.465	−0.012

注：营业收入、净利润、中位数调整后净利润单位为 10 亿元，保留 3 位小数。

根据表2描述，上市公司高管平均薪酬236 193.9元，高于方军雄(2009)根据2001—2007年样本的统计结果201 473.0元，由于本文选用1998—2010年样本，说明上市公司高管薪酬在持续走高。盈利的上市公司平均净利润为2.57亿元，高于方军雄(2009)的统计结果，说明上市公司净利润在持续增加。同时亏损的上市公司平均亏损为1.96亿元，最大亏损大约为91.49亿元。中位数调整后净利润通过年度公司利润与年度本行业中位数相减得到。行业采用证监会2001年颁布的分类标准，除制造业按照二级明细划分，其余行业按照一级行业划分。东部上市公司所占比例最大，西部公司最小，中部公司居中。同时发行A股和B股的公司大约占6.9%，董事长、总经理两职合一的公司大约占15.1%，大约64.7%的公司设立了薪酬考核委员会。

四、实证结果及分析

（一）薪酬激励的梯度效应实证结果

根据公式(1)按照净利润是否大于0分别进行回归，大于0为薪酬奖励样本，反之为薪酬惩罚样本，回归结果见表3、表4。通过表3可以发现：在薪酬奖励样本中，分别采用净利润和经过年度行业中位数调整后净利润为业绩的替代变量，业绩变量的系数β_1为正，统计上非常显著，表明随着业绩的增加高管薪酬增加。在其他条件相同的情况下，净利润增加10亿元，高管的薪酬增加4.2%，说明薪酬契约是解决代理问题的途径之一。同时业绩的平方系数β_2为负，统计上非常显著。不管采用净利润还是经过行业年度中位数调整后的净利润均得到相同的结果，证明了薪酬激励存在梯度效应。在没有梯度效应情况下，净利润增加10亿元，高管薪酬增加4.2%，存在梯度效应情况下，净利润增加10亿元，高管薪酬增加4.17%(0.042－0.000 3)，基本上没有差别；但是当净利润增加100亿元时，在没有梯度效应情况下，高管薪酬增加42%，而有梯度效应情况下，高管薪酬只能增加39%(0.042×10－0.000 3×100)，表明随着业绩的增加，高管薪酬奖励逐渐减少。经过行业中位数调整后的净利润的回归结果更加明显。在其他条件相同的情况下，没有梯度效应时，净利润超过年度行业中位数10亿元，高管薪酬增加117.1%，而存在梯度效应时，高管薪酬只增加74.9%(1.171－0.422)。实证结果说明薪酬业绩敏感性是随着业绩增加的一个变量。这种结果有利于公司在激励高管追求利润的同时不过分追求利润，

表 3　薪酬奖励梯度效应回归结果　　n=11 414

变量	净利润		中位数调整后净利润	
	参数估计值	T 值	参数估计值	T 值
业绩	0.042***	5.22	1.171***	19.75
业绩的平方	−0.000 3***	−4.52	−0.422***	−14.52
国企	−0.146***	−8.65	−0.148***	−8.88
第一大股东持股	−0.162***	−9.84	−0.185***	−11.44
西部	−0.101***	−4.62	−0.102***	−4.77
东部	0.151***	9.55	0.143***	9.20
B股	0.164***	5.67	0.135***	4.74
两职合一	0.097***	4.75	0.107***	5.30
独董比例	−0.023	−0.43	−0.031	−0.58
薪酬考核委员会	0.175***	8.77	0.176***	8.98
营业收入	0.180***	35.04	0.130***	23.35
资产负债率	−0.209***	−4.93	−0.102**	−2.43
行业	控制		控制	
年度	控制		控制	
截距	6.813***	8.75	7.670***	10.02
	Adj R-squared=0.383		Adj R-squared=0.406 0	

注：第2、3列采用净利润作为业绩指标。第4、5列采用经过行业中位数调整的净利润作为业绩指标。净利润、中位数调整后净利润单位为10亿元。高管薪酬、营业收入取对数处理。参数估计值保留3位小数。* $p<0.1$；** $p<0.05$；*** $p<0.01$。

有利于抑制公司经营风险，同时委托人也付出更低的薪酬，降低了代理成本。控制变量国企、大股东持股比例、西部上市公司、资产负债率系数为负，说明国企高管薪酬更低，大股东持股比例越高高管薪酬越低，西部公司高管薪酬更低，资产负债率越高高管薪酬越低；东部上市公司、同时发行B股、两职合一、薪酬委员会、营业收入系数为正，说明东部上市公司高管薪酬更高，同时发行B股的公司高管薪酬更高，董事长总经理合二为一的公司高管薪酬更高，存在薪酬委员会的公司高管薪酬更高，营业收入越高公司高管薪酬越高。而独立董事比例变量结果不显著。以上结果与方军雄(2009)的回归结果基本一致，说明回归结果基本可信。

表 4　薪酬惩罚梯度效应回归结果　　$n=1\,302$

变量	净利润		中位数调整后净利润	
	参数估计值	T 值	参数估计值	T 值
业绩	−0.670***	−2.78	−2.769***	−3.86
业绩的平方	−0.523***	−2.73	−4.818***	−3.38
国企	−0.231***	−4.80	−0.238***	−4.95
第一大股东持股	−0.077	−1.60	−0.072	−1.50
西部	−0.059	−1.05	−0.054	−0.97
东部	0.238***	5.13	0.241***	5.22
B 股	0.266***	3.27	0.263***	3.25
两职合一	0.181***	3.08	0.176***	3.01
独董比例	−0.301*	−1.95	−0.296*	−1.92
薪酬考核委员会	0.264***	4.84	0.257***	4.73
营业收入	0.068***	7.90	0.067***	7.83
资产负债率	−0.134	−1.20	−0.166	−1.48
行业	控制		控制	
年度	控制		控制	
截距	8.897***	22.27	8.752***	21.87
	Adj R-squared=0.3460		Adj R-squared=0.3504	

注：第 2、3 列采用净利润作为业绩指标。第 4、5 列采用经过行业中位数调整的净利润作为业绩指标。净利润、中位数调整后净利润单位为 10 亿元。高管薪酬、营业收入取对数处理。参数估计值保留 3 位小数。* $p<0.1$；** $p<0.05$；*** $p<0.01$。

在薪酬惩罚样本中，分别采用净利润和经过行业年度中位数调整后净利润作为业绩指标，回归结果见表 4。[9] 业绩指标的系数 β_2 为负，统计上非常显著，说明随着亏损程度的增加高管会受到边际递增的薪酬惩罚。β_1 系数为正，与假设相反，亏损越多薪酬反而越高不太符合常理。由于 β_2 系数是乘以业绩的平方，β_2 系数的影响远远大于 β_1 系数，导致总的影响 $\beta_1+\beta_2$ 迅速变大。因此，总体上高管会因为亏损程度的加大受到边际递增的惩罚。经过行业中位数调整后的净利润回归结果相同。在其他条件相同情况下，没有梯度效应，亏损增加 10 亿元，高管薪酬增加 67%，存在梯度效应，薪酬只增加 14.7%。亏损继续增加，高管薪酬就会出现累积递增的减少。净利润亏损超过年度行业中位数 10 亿元，高管薪酬增加 276.9%，而存在梯度效应情况下，高管薪酬减少 204.9%

[9] 本文研究建立在薪酬业绩相关基础上。在回归中为了减少薪酬业绩不相关异常值的影响，剔除亏损样本中十分位数最小 10%、薪酬十分位数最高 10% 的样本 34 个；亏损十分位数最大 10%、薪酬十分位数最小 10% 的样本 9 个，即剔除极端亏损最多、薪酬最高和亏损最少、薪酬最低样本。

(－4.818×12－2.769×(－1))。从计算结果来看,说明梯度效应因素非常重要。实证结果 β_1 系数不是很理想,需要在今后的研究中继续探讨。控制变量上差别不大,值得注意的是独董比例变量统计上变显著。

通过表3、表4证明了假设1薪酬契约具有梯度效应。具体而言,在实现盈利的情况下,高管获得的薪酬奖励随着业绩的增加边际递减;在亏损情况下,高管获得的薪酬惩罚随着亏损程度的加大边际递增。方军雄(2009)发现业绩上升时薪酬的增加幅度显著高于业绩下降时薪酬的减少幅度,认为高管的薪酬存在粘性特征。该研究仅仅考虑净利润大于0的样本,本文发现在出现亏损情况下,高管会受到更加严厉的薪酬惩罚,说明薪酬的"粘性"特征有不成立的时候。

(二)行业性质的梯度效应实证结果

根据假设2,行业特征的不同导致薪酬契约的梯度效应存在差异。垄断企业的定义采用我国上市公司高管薪酬指数报告的方法。按照HHI指数计算结果认定采掘业、水电煤气业、金融保险业、电信业、铁路建筑业、民航业、远洋运输业为垄断行业。本文以此为依据,认定上述企业为垄断企业,其值取1,其余为0。根据国家高新技术产品目录将电子信息、航空航天、生物、医药和医疗器械、地球、空间与海洋等行业定义为高科技行业。高科技企业取值为1,反之为0。计算结果见表5:高科技企业约占上市公司的16%,垄断企业约占上市公司的6%,垄断企业全部为国企。

表5　行业效应梯度效应回归结果

变量名	样本数	均值	标准差	最小值	最大值
高科技	12816	0.160	0.367	0	1
垄断	12816	0.060	0.238	0	1

注:保留3位小数。

在根据公式(2)的回归中,为了避免共线性问题剔除国企变量。同时考虑高科技行业以及垄断行业亏损企业样本很少,研究中仅仅考虑薪酬奖励忽略薪酬惩罚,净利润小于0的样本全部剔除,回归结果见表6和表7。如果不是垄断企业,净利润指标的系数 β_1 为0.269,统计上显著,表明随着业绩的增加,高管的薪酬增加;同时净利润的平方系数 β_2 为负,证明了薪酬激励存在梯度效应,随着业绩的增加,敏感性系数变小。变量 D(垄断)与业绩交乘项为负,与业绩平方的交乘项为正,统计上显著。与其他行业相比,如果是垄断行业,净利润的系数变成 0.006(0.269－0.263),说明垄断行业的薪酬业绩敏感性更低;同时净利润的平方系数变成 0(－0.015＋0.015),基本不存在梯度效应。回归结果与假设相符,垄断行业的特征决定了与其他行业相比不需要太多的薪酬激励,梯度效应自然不存在。经过年度行业中位数调整后的净利润作为业绩替代变量得到的结果相近。

表 6 垄断行业梯度效应回归结果 n=12 795

	净利润		中位数调整后净利润	
垄断行业	参数估计值	T 值	参数估计值	T 值
业绩	0.269***	14.65	1.201***	23.34
业绩的平方	－0.015***	－8.20	－0.400***	－14.66
垄断企业	－0.110	－0.14	－0.100	－0.13
D×业绩	－0.263***	－12.95	－0.833***	－6.62
D×业绩的平方	0.015***	8.19	0.282***	4.36
第一大股东持股	－0.170***	－11.04	－0.194***	－12.75
西部	－0.100***	－4.86	－0.107***	－5.26
东部	0.183***	12.14	0.173***	11.72
B 股	0.150***	5.45	0.136***	5.05
两职合一	0.125***	6.44	0.132***	6.91
独董比例	－0.012	－0.24	－0.024	－0.48
薪酬考核委员会	0.178***	9.44	0.180***	9.71
营业收入	0.145***	33.73	0.114***	25.58
资产负债率	－0.229***	－5.95	－0.087**	－2.27
行业、年度		控制		
截距	7.484***	9.54	7.999***	10.36
	Adj R-squared＝0.383 7		Adj R-squared＝0.404 6	

注:参数估计值保留 3 位小数。* $p<0.1$; ** $p<0.05$; *** $p<0.01$。净利润的计算单位为 10 亿元。

表 7 高科技行业梯度效应回归结果 n=12 795

	净利润		中位数调整后净利润	
高科技行业	参数估计值	T 值	参数估计值	T 值
业绩	0.055***	6.85	1.031***	20.51
业绩的平方	－0.0004***	－5.89	－0.345***	－13.27
高科技企业	0.537	0.97	0.540	1.00
D×业绩	0.324***	4.96	0.423***	3.10
D×业绩的平方	－0.021***	－5.51	－0.230***	－2.86
第一大股东持股	－0.167***	－10.78	－0.196***	－12.87
西部	－0.097***	－4.69	－0.098***	－4.85

（续表）

高科技行业	净利润		中位数调整后净利润	
	参数估计值	T 值	参数估计值	T 值
东部	0.180***	11.88	0.171***	11.56
B股	0.161***	5.82	0.142***	5.24
两职合一	0.121***	6.22	0.131***	6.86
独董比例	0.001	0.02	−0.017	−0.35
薪酬考核委员会	0.174***	9.15	0.176***	9.46
营业收入	0.153***	35.96	0.116***	26.09
资产负债率	−0.263***	−6.83	−0.089**	−2.32
行业、年度	控制			
截距	7.348***	9.31	7.956***	10.29
	Adj R-squared=0.377 1		Adj R-squared=0.402 1	

注：参数估计值保留3位小数。* $p<0.1$；** $p<0.05$；*** $p<0.01$。净利润的计算单位为10亿元。

同样，高科技企业净利润的系数为0.055，统计上显著，表明随着业绩的增加，高管的薪酬增加；同时净利润的平方系数 β_2 为−0.000 4，统计上显著，证明了薪酬激励存在梯度效应，随着业绩的增加，敏感性系数变小。高科技企业的行业与净利润交乘项为正，与净利润平方的交乘项为负，统计上显著。与其他行业相比，高科技企业的薪酬业绩敏感性更强，为0.379(0.055+0.324)，说明高科技企业的代理问题更严重，需要用更高的薪酬激励来解决代理问题。因此，高科技企业薪酬业绩敏感性系数较高。净利润的平方系数变成−0.214(−0.000 4−0.021)，高科技企业的风险更大，需要在薪酬契约中采用更强的梯度效应来控制经营风险，证明了高科技行业中薪酬契约存在更强的梯度效应。其余控制变量符号没有变化。

五、稳健性检验

在前文中，笔者构建二次函数回归模型研究薪酬契约的梯度效应，为了增强文章的稳健性，笔者重新构建模型(3)检验薪酬契约中的梯度效应：

$$\text{Comp} = \alpha + \beta_1 \text{performance} + \beta_2 \text{cdf} + \beta_3 \text{cdf} \times \text{performance} + \text{Control variable} + \text{indus} + \text{years} + \varepsilon \quad (3)$$

其中，performance表示业绩，用净利润和经过行业年度中位数调整过的净利润作为替代变量。cdf表示标准化处理后(均值为0，方差为1)的净利润或者经过年度行业中位数调整后净利润的累积概率密度函数。控制变量选择与前文相同。对公式(3)求一阶偏导得到：dcomp/dperformance$=\beta_1+\beta_3$cdf。cdf变量从

0到1改变对应业绩从最小到最大转变。相应的业绩最小的时候，cdf＝0，薪酬业绩敏感性系数为β_1，而业绩最好的时候，cdf＝1，薪酬业绩敏感性系数为$\beta_1+\beta_3$。当业绩处于中间位置时，薪酬业绩敏感性系数为$\beta_1+0.5\beta_3$。根据假设1，薪酬奖励样本，β_1为正，表明业绩越好薪酬越高；β_3为负，表明薪酬业绩敏感性随业绩的增加而下降。反之，薪酬惩罚样本，β_1为正，表明亏损越多薪酬越低；β_3为负，表明薪酬业绩敏感性随亏损的增加而加强。

与前文一致，通过表8结果发现与假设1相符，业绩的系数为正，业绩×cdf的系数为负。不管是采用净利润还是经过行业年度调整后的净利润作为业绩的替代变量，统计上均显著，说明对于薪酬奖励样本，薪酬契约具有梯度效应，薪酬业绩敏感性系数随业绩的增加而下降。

表8　薪酬奖励梯度效应稳健性检验　　n＝11 414

变量	净利润		中位数调整后净利润	
	参数估计值	T值	参数估计值	T值
业绩	1.939***	15.46	1.967***	7.41
cdf	0.034	0.17	0.766***	7.34
业绩×cdf	−1.929***	−15.53	−1.920***	−7.94
国企	−0.150***	−9.00	−0.144***	−8.68
第一大股东持股	−0.182***	−11.24	−0.190***	−11.78
西部	−0.108***	−5.01	−0.096***	−4.48
东部	0.143***	9.20	0.139***	9.00
B股	0.136***	4.78	0.135***	4.76
两职合一	0.103***	5.13	0.108***	5.42
独董比例	−0.027	−0.52	−0.033	−0.64
薪酬考核委员会	0.179***	9.13	0.169***	8.68
营业收入	0.131***	23.54	0.119***	21.08
资产负债率	−0.111***	−2.65	−0.075*	−1.81
行业	控制		控制	
年度	控制		控制	
截距	7.620***	9.89	7.561***	9.92
	Adj R-squared＝0.405		Adj R-squared＝0.412 1	

注：第2、3列采用净利润作为业绩指标。第4、5列采用经过行业中位数调整的净利润作为业绩指标。净利润、中位数调整后净利润单位为10亿元。高管薪酬、营业收入取对数处理。参数估计值保留3位小数。* $p<0.1$；** $p<0.05$；*** $p<0.01$。

通过表9结果发现与假设1相符，业绩的系数为正，业绩×cdf的系数为负。采用净利润作为业绩的替代变量，统计上显著。说明对于薪酬惩罚样本，薪酬契约具有梯度效应，薪酬业绩敏感性系数随亏损的增加而增加。经过行业年度调整后的净利润作为业绩的替代变量，统计上不显著，同样在薪酬惩罚样本中，独立董事作用明显。其余控制变量变化不大。

表 9　薪酬惩罚梯度效应稳健性检验　n=1 302

变量	净利润		中位数调整后净利润	
	参数估计值	T 值	参数估计值	T 值
业绩	0.125	0.52	1.505	1.46
cdf	−0.277	−1.16	−0.925**	−2.27
业绩×cdf	−2.201**	−2.07	−1.198	−0.95
国企	−0.236***	−4.90	−0.237***	−4.94
第一大股东持股	−0.074	−1.55	−0.071	−1.48
西部	−0.057	−1.03	−0.054	−0.97
东部	0.240***	5.20	0.240***	5.21
B 股	0.264***	3.25	0.265***	3.27
两职合一	0.180***	3.06	0.177***	3.02
独董比例	−0.303*	−1.96	−0.300*	−1.95
薪酬考核委员会	0.260***	4.77	0.258***	4.74
营业收入	0.067***	7.77	0.067***	7.84
资产负债率	−0.161	−1.43	−0.163	−1.46
行业	控制		控制	
年度	控制		控制	
截距	9.069***	20.15	9.672***	16.72
	Adj R-squared=0.348 1		Adj R-squared=0.350 3	

注：第 2、3 列采用净利润作为业绩指标。第 4、5 列采用经过行业中位数调整的净利润作为业绩指标。净利润、中位数调整后净利润的单位为 10 亿元。高管薪酬、营业收入取对数处理。参数估计值保留 3 位小数。* $p<0.1$； ** $p<0.05$； *** $p<0.01$。

六、结　　论

高管薪酬与企业经营业绩相关，有利于缓解风险规避和自我利益最大化的高管与股东的利益冲突，提高企业经营效益。本文研究发现薪酬业绩仅仅线性相关不够，这种相关还要伴随业绩、行业特征的变化而改变。在盈利情况下，薪酬业绩敏感性呈现边际递减的梯度效应，而亏损公司的薪酬业绩敏感性呈现边际递增的梯度效应。垄断行业基本不存在梯度效应，而高科技行业梯度效应较强。本文研究结论验证了从薪酬契约中静态的薪酬业绩敏感性到薪酬业绩关系梯度效应动态特征的变化，契约的制定越来越精细，对代理人的引导更加精准，在降低代理成本的功效上更加明显。

参考文献

[1] 杜兴强、王丽华,2007,高层管理当局薪酬与上市公司业绩的相关性实证研究,《会计研究》,第1期,第58—65页。

[2] 方军雄,2009,我国上市公司高管的薪酬存在粘性吗?《经济研究》,第3期,第110—124页。

[3] 刘洪军,2004,惩罚与宽恕的经济学分析——机会主义与制度变迁,《制度经济学研究》,第1期,第128—143页。

[4] 刘斌、刘星、李世新、何顺文,2003,CEO薪酬与企业业绩互动效应的实证检验,《会计研究》,第3期,第35—39页。

[5] 威廉·R.斯科特,2006,《实证会计理论》,陈汉文、夏文贤、陈靖译,北京:机械工业出版社。

[6] Aggarwal, R. K. and Samwick, A. A., 1999, Executive compensation, strategic competition, and relative performance evaluation: Theory and evidence, *The Journal of Finance*, Vol. 6, pp. 2 000—2 043.

[7] Armen, A. A., 1950, Uncertainty, evolution, and economic theory, *Journal of Political Economy*, Vol. 58, pp. 211—221.

[8] Arvey, R. D., Davis, G. A. and Nelson, S. M., 1984, Use of discipline in an organization: A field study, *J. Appl. Psych*, Vol. 69, pp. 448—460.

[9] Garvey, G. T. and Milbourn, T. T., 2006, Asymmetric benchmarking in compensation: Executives are rewarded for good luck but not penalized for bad, *Journal of Financial Economics*, Vol. 82, pp. 197—225.

[10] Gray, S. R. and Cannella, A. A., 1997, The role of risk in executive compensation, *Journal of Management*, Vol. 23, pp. 517—540.

[11] Healy, P. M., 1985, The effect of bonus schemes on accounting decisions, *Journal of Accounting & Economics*, Vol. 7, pp. 85—107.

[12] Jensen, M. C. and Meckling, W. H., 1976, Theory of the firm: Managerial behavior, agency costs and ownership structure, *Journal of Finance Economics*, Vol. 3, pp. 305—360.

[13] Jensen, M. and Murphy, K., 1999, Performance pay and top-management incentives, *Journal of Political Economy*, Vol. 98, pp. 225—264.

[14] Joskow, P. L., Rose, N. L. and Wolfram, C. D., 1996, Political constraints on executive compensation: Evidence from the electric utility industry, *The RAND Journal of Economics*, Vol. 27, pp. 165—182.

[15] Lambert, R. A., 2001, Contracting theory and accounting, *Journal of accounting and economics*, Vol. 32, pp. 3—87.

[16] MacCrimmon, K. and Donald, A. W., 1986, *Taking Risks: The Management of Uncertainty*, Free Press, New York.

[17] Mark, C. A. and Banker, D. ,2000, Executive compensation in the information technology industry, *Management Science*, Vol. 46, pp. 530—547.

[18] Murphy, K. J. , 1999, Executive compensation, *Handbook of Labor Economics*, Vol. 3, pp. 2 485—2 563.

[19] Randolph, P. B. and Edward, J. Z. , 1994, Managerial incentives, monitoring, and risk bearing: A study of executive compensation, ownership, and board structure in initial public offerings, *Administrative Science Quarterly*, Vol. 39, pp. 313—325.

[20] Shaw, K. W. and Zhang, M. H. , 2010, Is CEO cash compensation punished for poor firm performance, *The Accounting Review*, Vol. 85, pp. 1 065—1 093.

[21] Smith, C. W. and Stulz, R. M. , 1985, The determinants of firms' hedging policies, *Journal of Financial and Quantitative Analysis*, Vol. 20, pp. 391—405.

[22] Xue, Y. , 2007, Make or buy new technology: The role of CEO compensation contract in a firm's route to innovation, *Review of Accounting Studies*, Vol. 12, pp. 659—690.

The Gradient Effect in Executive Compensation Incentives of Chinese Listed Companies

TAO JIANG

(*Chongqing University of Technology*)

YUNGUO LIU

(*Sun Yat-sen University*)

Abstract Based on the 1998—2010 data of Chinese listed companies, we find that compensation contracts have the gradient effect. Pay-performance sensitivity decreases with the increasing performance in the profitable business. On the contrary, pay-performance sensitivity increases with the increasing loss. Monopolies do not have the gradient effect, but the effect is strong in high-tech companies. This study suggests that more accurate and detailed compensation contracts can reduce the agency cost.

Key words Executive Compensation Contract, Gradient Effect, Industry Characteristics

环境不确定性、公司战略、组织结构对预算控制紧度的影响
——基于中国中小企业的调查研究

于李胜 江 权*

摘 要 本文通过对 210 份有效问卷进行分析，深入讨论了环境不确定性、战略、组织结构对预算控制紧度的影响。我们的研究结论是：环境不确定性越高、实施差异化战略的企业的预算控制紧度越低，组织分权程度越高以及实施成本领先战略的企业预算控制紧度越高。我们还发现成本领先战略对预算控制紧度的影响最大；组织分权程度受到环境不确定性、战略的影响，在环境不确定性、战略对预算控制紧度的影响中起着重要的中介作用。

关键词 预算控制紧度，战略，环境不确定性，组织分权程度

一、引 言

控制功能是预算管理的基本功能之一。在过去几十年，狭义的管理控制就是指预算控制。而控制功能的一个重要特征是控制紧度。Merchant(1985a)认为控制紧度是能够全面概括企业总体控制思想的少数几个宏观控制概念之一。因此，研究控制紧度对于理解公司的管理控制系统有着重要的作用。国外的学

* 于李胜（通信作者），厦门大学管理学院会计系与会计发展研究中心，通信地址：厦门大学管理学院会计系，邮编：361005，E-mail：yulisheng@xmu.edu.cn；江权，江苏方天电力技术有限公司，E-mail：356187499@qq.com。作者感谢国家自然科学基金项目（71002043、70972114）、教育部新世纪优秀人才（NCET-11-0297）、福建省新世纪优秀人才和霍英东青年教师基金（131083）、中央高校基本科研业务费项目“非金融企业套期保值行为及监管模式研究”、“审计师个体行为特征与审计质量研究”以及教育部人文社科重点基地重大项目（2009JJD790041）的资助。本文选自中国会计学会管理会计分委员会 2012 年会论文，文章由胡玉明教授接收。

者针对预算控制紧度展开了深入的研究(Merchant,1985b;Chow et al.,1996;Anthony and Govindarajan,1998;Stede,2001),然而国内相关研究甚少,只有鲍卫新(2008)、郑石桥(2008)等做了初步的尝试。本文主要从预算控制紧度的影响因素出发,从环境不确定性、战略、组织分权程度等角度研究对预算控制紧度的影响,对比了各影响因素的影响程度大小,并描绘出相应的影响路径。

我们研究的意义在于:首先,我们的研究补充和完善了蔡剑辉(2009)的研究,他认为,传统预算模式下,预算既担负着计划、协调和资源分配等决策职能,又是业绩评价和薪酬激励的标准,以及成本控制系统的一部分。这种不加区分的、不恰当的使用预算的行为,会导致预算职能之间的冲突,并引发一系列的功能紊乱。然而我们的研究表明,以低成本战略为主导的企业预算控制紧度比较强,而以差异化战略为主导、外部环境不确定性高、组织分权程度高的企业更倾向于预算松控制。这说明企业会根据外部环境不确定性的大小,通过实施何种战略以及调整组织的分权程度等,对预算控制的紧度进行调节。这也暗示了企业在运用预算管理工具时,不会简单地混合使用,而是对于预算的控制和决策职能进行有选择的倚重。

其次,我们利用结构方程(SEM)对于环境不确定性、战略以及组织分权程度对预算控制紧度的影响同时进行估计。我们的研究表明,组织分权程度不是一个外生变量,本身受到外部环境和公司战略的影响,在环境和战略对预算控制紧度影响中起到重要的中介作用。而国内过去关于组织分权程度对于预算特征的影响的相关研究未考虑其内生性问题(如郑石桥,2008),我们的研究修正了这些理论。

最后,本文基于我国新兴加转型背景下企业预算控制紧度影响因素的研究,弥补了新兴市场中关于预算控制紧度研究的文献。过去的研究主要关注西方发达国家,这些国家的企业对于预算的使用和探索已有近百年的历史,相关的实践和研究结果是否在发展中国家适用,特别是在我国这样一个新兴加转型的国家适用,没有相应的文献支持,我们的研究填补了这方面的空白。

我们的研究结论是:环境不确定性越高、实施差异化战略的企业的预算控制紧度越低,组织分权程度越高以及实施成本领先战略的企业预算控制紧度越高。我们还发现成本领先战略对预算控制紧度的影响最大,同时,组织分权程度受到环境不确定性、战略的影响,在环境不确定性、战略对预算控制紧度的影响中起着重要的中介作用。

本文后续安排如下：第二部分是关于预算控制紧度的相关文献回顾，以及根据过去的研究文献提出相应的假说；第三部分是研究设计，主要是针对问卷的基本情况进行描述分析，对于主要变量衡量进行解释；第四部分实证检验，主要是通过对问卷的信度、效度检验，进行结构方程分析，验证假说；第五部分是结论与讨论，主要是总结全文的研究结论，并针对本文的结论进行深入的讨论。

二、文献回顾与假说发展

Merchant(1985a)认为控制紧度是能够全面概括企业总体控制思想的少数几个宏观控制概念之一。然而，现有的研究中并没有针对紧控制进行准确的定义，这成为困扰学者多年的问题(Simons,1995)。识别和计量预算紧控制及其组成部分，已经成为学术界一个重要的研究领域(Chow et al.,1996)。Anthony and Govindarajan(1998)在关于管理控制系统的研究中将紧控制描述为在每一个报告期，管理者的业绩主要是基于能否完成预算目标进行考核，即预算紧控制是通过预算过程实现的，例如强调预算目标的完成。然而，Merchant(1985b)认为，紧控制意味着对个体自由程度严厉的限制，但是无须每个月分析预算执行的细节，并针对预算目标的完成情况进行业绩评价。进一步的，文献中又引入与紧控制相关的其他控制系统，如诊断式控制(Simons,1995)和管理控制(Merchant,1981)。一些学者通过分解预算紧控制的组成部分(Anthony and Govindarajan,1998)，或者是从实现紧控制的过程角度描述紧控制(Merchant,1985b)，还有一些学者从控制的后果来推测紧控制(Merchant,1985a,1990)。比如，从控制后果来衡量，如果一个控制系统是紧控制，那么对决策会有更大的影响(Merchant,1985a,1990)，或者员工行为与组织的愿望保持更高程度的一致(Merchant,1990)。本文借鉴Stede(2001)的研究，主要从预算目标的刚性衡量预算控制紧度，深入探讨环境、战略、组织结构对预算控制紧度的影响。

(一) 环境的不确定性和预算控制紧度

传统的关于不确定性和预算的关系的研究结论一直很模糊(Hopwood,1980;Dent,1986)。权变理论认为管理控制系统依赖于特定的环境或组织的运营情况(Otley,1980;Dent,1986;Chenhall and Morris,1986;Briers and Hirst,

1990)。一个组织要有效地运行,其组织结构和控制系统必须与其环境相适应。因而,在不同环境下,其预算方式会不同,预算控制的紧度也将有所不同。而预算作为一种信息处理形式,是用来减少这种管理的不确定性。所以,在环境不确定的情况下,管理者需要花费更多的时间去了解组织的外部环境,并对外部环境做出合理和相对准确的预测,以使企业能够积极面对外部环境的变化。Fitzgerald et al. (1991)认为在企业面临不确定环境的情形下,对预算的最好的使用是了解并与适当层次的管理层沟通外部环境的变化。但是,环境变化越不确定,我们越难精确而且自信地说明环境的状况。在环境高度不确定的情形下,预算系统甚至变得不适合作为控制和业绩评价的手段(Chenhall and Morris,1986;Govindarajan,1984;Gordon and Narayanan,1984;Fitzgerald et al.,1991),因为最初的预算标准已经变得过时且不相关。同时,在环境高度不确定性的情况下,预算作为业绩评价工具将带来如下恶果:压力和失常的行为等(Merchant,1990)。所以,来自组织环境的不确定性可能会影响到组织的预算过程(Otley,1978),环境的复杂性(来自供应商和政府)和预算强调的减少是相关的(Brownell,1985)。因此,我们可以推测随着外部环境不确定性的增强,预算控制紧度会减弱。然而在我国,企业的预算控制系统深受计划经济的影响,预算对外界环境的应变能力还十分有限,企业管理者是否会根据外部环境的变化调整预算控制紧度,这是一个需要实证检验的问题,为此,我们提出假设1:

假设1　在其他条件相同的情况下,随着环境不确定性的增强,预算控制紧度减弱。

(二)环境的不确定性与组织分权程度

环境的不确定性和组织结构的关系已经得到人们的广泛了解。环境越不确定,组织越分权,组织对环境的变化越可以做出积极的反应。Khandwalla (1972)和Duncan(1971)发现组织的分权程度和环境的竞争程度呈正相关关系。环境越动荡,组织的分权程度越高(Lawrence and Lorsch,1967;Leifer and Huber,1978;Gordon and Narayanan,1984);环境越不可预测,组织的分权程度越高(Gordon and Miller,1976;Waterhouse and Tiessen,1978;Gordon and Narayanan,1984)。在我国,随着全球经济一体化进程的逐步深入,企业所面临的外部环境的不确定性越来越高,特别是金融危机的影响意味着企业必须在组织结构上重新调整以满足外部环境多变的需要,基于上述分析,我们提出假设2：

假设2 在其他条件相同的情况下，随着环境不确定性的增强，组织分权程度增大。

（三）战略定位和预算控制紧度

直到20世纪80年代，战略才成为管理控制系统研究的一个变量。近年来，人们对管理控制系统和战略之间关系研究的兴趣越来越浓厚。管理控制系统只有和战略紧密配合，才能发挥竞争优势，并给企业带来更高的业绩（Dent，1990；Samson et al.，1991；Simons，1987，1990）。关于战略的定义，目前尚不统一。本文采用战略大师迈克尔·波特先生对战略的理解，将战略分为成本领先战略和差异化战略两种。根据波特的观点（Porter，1980，1985），采用成本领先战略的企业有如下特征：(1) 积极寻求成本的减少；(2) 雇用有经验的员工并实施所有可能的规模经济；(3) 拥有高效率生产的能力；(4) 使任务环境日常化；(5) 生产标准、无差异的产品。差异化战略的关键成功因素是创造性眼光、强大的基础研究、产品工程（Porter，1980），这些成功因素的实现意味着无法准确地衡量短期产出，使得产出控制变得不合适（Ouchi，1979）。

追求差异化战略的企业试图生产出独一无二的产品，这使得关于方法和目的的相关知识变得不重要，并且生产和营销独一无二的产品意味着任务的程序化程度更低。最近的研究表明采取差异化战略的战略子单位（SBU）的任务环境比实施低成本战略的战略子单位的任务环境更不确定（Miller，1988）。

不同的战略面临不同程度的环境不确定性，不同程度的环境不确定性需要不同的控制和预算实务。战略是企业发展的方向，是企业未来走向的指引，有什么样的战略就应有相应的预算控制系统与其对应。Simons（1995）认为预算在追求低成本战略的组织中作为控制和业绩评价的工具可能更有效。Govindarajan（1988）发现，在追求差异化战略的组织中，对满足预算目标的较低强调是与更高的业绩表现相联系的。Van der Stede（2000）认为追求产品差异化战略的组织，预算控制较松，并将导致预算松弛的增加。所以采用成本领先战略的组织比采用差异化战略的组织更倾向于采用正式的业绩评价系统，用客观预算指标进行业绩评价。

国内关于预算与战略关系的研究尚少，郑石桥（2008）针对战略对预算功能的影响进行了研究，认为采用成本领先战略的企业更注重预算的目标沟通功能及战略细化功能，而对预算的综合计划功能及业绩评价功能需求较少；采取差异化战略的企业相对更注重预算的综合计划功能及业绩评价功能。根据上述回顾，我们提出以下假设3和假设4：

假设3　在其他条件相同的情况下，成本领先战略与预算控制紧度呈正向关系。

假设4　在其他条件相同的情况下，产品差异化战略与预算控制紧度呈负向关系。

（四）战略和组织分权程度

关于战略与组织结构之间的关系一直是理论界争论的热点问题。Chandler(1962)首次提出，战略是先于组织结构出现，公司应首先建立一套战略，然后摸索创建战略的结构，最后化为现实。Chandler的研究开创了战略关联领域的战略—结构—绩效范式。Child(1972)将Chandler的观点又向前推进了一步，指出管理人员会采取行动界定或操作其他组织领域，因此，可以不理会或抑制环境因素迫使现在组织结构改变的安排。然而Chandler的假设从20世纪70年代开始就不断受到质疑。Ansoff(1979)认为战略追随结构，战略管理过程是一个开放系统。然而，Drucker(1998)认为，不同组织的管理是有差异的，这是因为使命决定战略，战略决定结构。事实上，正如Besanko，Dranove and Shanley(1996)所指出的，结构与战略本身都是一些复杂的行为方式或常规的集合，而这些行为方式是在企业组织对外部环境不断做出反应的过程中逐步演化而来的。而且，为求从竞争中取胜，不同的企业常采取不同的战略，争取本身独特的优势。采用成本导向战略，就必须控制成本，并以此作为竞争优势，企业需要一个较为复杂的结构（即高度专业化、高度制度化而且中央集权的结构）去配合；采用差异化战略，必须提高弹性及应变能力，要求结构方面需要较低的复杂性、形式化程度及权力集中程度，留出较大的空间给员工，以促进组织内的创新(Robins，1990)。为此，我们提出如下假设：

假设5　在其他条件相同的情况下，成本领先战略与组织分权呈负向关系。

假设6　在其他条件相同的情况下，产品差异化战略与组织分权呈正向关系。

（五）组织分权程度与预算控制紧度

分权的组织更倾向于采用管理导向型控制(administrative oriented controls),在此情形下,企业更强调正式的控制机制(Bruns and Waterhouse,1975)。在企业的控制系统中,预算处于核心地位,因而分权的组织更强调预算在企业的控制作用。所以我们认为在分权的组织中预算控制相对于集权组织会更紧。

在一个分权的组织中,组织可以聚集和整合更多有用的信息(Chenhall and Morris,1986),组织可以利用这些信息及时做出反应。拥有精密技术的且分权的大型企业和对正式的管理控制系统的强烈强调是相关的(Bruns and Waterhouse,1975);大型、多样化且分权的企业使用更多的管理控制(强调预算、精细的预算、正式的交流类型和预算参与的重要性)(Merchant,1981)。管理业绩和分权与广泛的、整合的、聚集的和及时来自管理控制系统的信息相互作用相关(Chia,1995)。拥有精密技术且多样化的大型分权组织与更加正式且传统的管理控制系统(如预算、正式的交流)是相关的(Chenhall,2003)。

集权组织可以对非程序化事项直接施加决策制定的影响来控制企业(Ramamurthy,1990),在集权组织中,标准和正式的程序是企业整合和控制的充分工具(Mintzberg,1979)。而在分权组织中,标准和正式的程序已无法满足企业控制的需要,预算作为一种控制系统,取代标准和程序来实施对企业的控制。研究表明,在分权组织中,人们对预算目标设置的参与更多,对满足预算目标的重要性更加强调,并更多地使用预算;而在集权组织中,管理者认为预算是无用的,预算限制了他们的灵活性。

因而,在分权组织中,预算作为正式控制系统的一种形式,企业会更多地通过预算进行控制和业绩评价(Sharma,2002)。在一个高度分权的组织中,可以预期的是对预算目标实现的强调和对预算的重视是比较强烈的,由此提出以下假设:

假设7 在其他情况相同的条件下,组织分权程度越高,预算控制紧度越高。

根据以上假设,我们构建环境不确定性、低成本战略、差异化战略、组织分权程度对预算控制紧度影响的路径模型,如图1所示,其中环境不确定性(PEU)、低成本战略(CS)、差异化战略(DS)是自变量,组织分权程度(DEC)是中介变量,预算控制紧度(BE)是因变量。

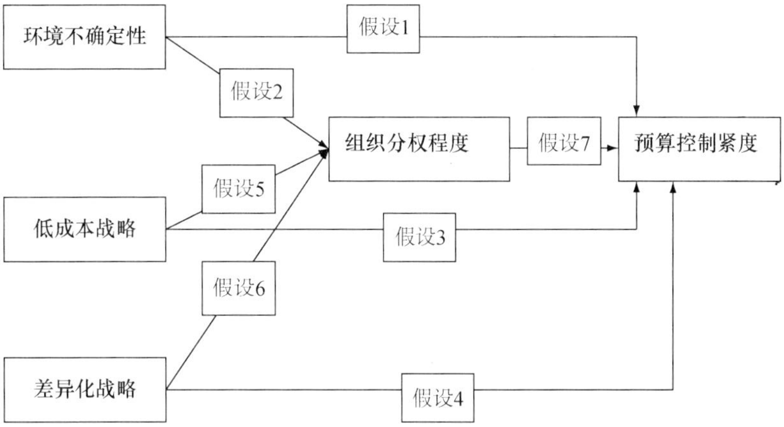

图 1　假设路径模型

三、研究设计

（一）研究方法

本研究主要采用调查问卷收集数据。问卷由环境不确定性、组织结构、预算功能、预算实践、预算特点、预算强调、战略等七部分组成。量表参考是在修订国内外相关量表的基础上（Sharma，2002；Zuriekat，Khadra and Alramahi，2009；郑石桥，2008），通过与企业内部各个层面的人员进行访谈[1]，修订量表。我们的问卷调查对象主要是 EMBA、EDP、MPAcc 的学员，共计发放 360 份问卷，调查时间从 2009 年 4 月至 2010 年 4 月，共回收问卷 257 份。对于数据缺失严重或回答跌入陷阱的，我们进行了剔除。一共剔除了 47 份问卷，最后得到有效问卷 210 份。问卷回收率是 71.4%，有效问卷回收率为 58.3%。

回收的有效问卷中，年龄在 30—39 岁占比最大，达到 42.4%，工作年限主要分布在 11—20 年，占比达到 53.3%，这些说明我们的调查对象具有较充足的工作经验，对于预算作为控制系统有深刻的体会。调查对象中中高层占比最多，达到 66.2%；另外，调查对象的教育程度分布中，本科及以上学历达到

[1] 作者利用参与某上市公司内部控制机制设计横向课题的机会，与企业的各个层级员工就本研究的相关问题进行沟通，进一步对问卷进行了修正。

94.3%，说明我们的调查对象具有一定的管理经验和良好的教育背景，这为他们很好地理解我们的问题，认识企业的环境、战略、组织结构以及预算的控制紧度提供了保障。被调查的企业中，国有企业占76.2%，民营企业占14.3%，外资企业占8.1%。具体结果见表1。

表1 问卷基本特征描述性分析

特征	分类	样本	百分比
性别	男	110	52.4%
	女	100	47.6%
年龄	20—29	43	20.5%
	30—39	89	42.4%
	40—49	39	18.55%
	50以上	39	18.55%
职位	普通员工	34	16.2%
	基层管理者	37	17.6%
	中层	66	31.4%
	高层	73	34.8%
教育程度	高中(职)以下	4	1.9%
	专科	8	3.8%
	本科	192	91.4%
	研究生及以上	6	2.9%
工作年限	1—2年	0	0
	3—5年	39	18.6%
	6—10年	45	21.4%
	11—20年	112	53.3%
	21年以上	14	6.7%
单位性质	国有企业	160	76.2%
	民营企业	30	14.3%
	外资企业	17	8.1%
	其他	3	1.4%
所在行业	制造业	55	26.2%
	服务业	118	56.2%
	其他	37	17.6%

（二）变量测度

1. 环境不确定性

关于环境不确定性的测度，我们参考了Gordon and Narayanan(1984)以及Khandwalla(1972,1977)的方法，这里主要从宏观调控政策、科技创新以及消费者偏好变化等三个方面测度，问题分值从1—5，其中1代表环境不确定性最弱的情形，5代表环境不确定性最强的情形。

2. 组织分权程度

关于组织分权程度的测度，我们借鉴了 Zuriekat, Khadra and Alramahi (2009)的问卷，主要从产品或服务开发、管理人员的聘用、投资、预算等四个问题测度。问题分值从 1—5，其中 1 代表组织分权程度最弱的情形，5 代表组织分权程度最强的情形。

3. 战略

关于战略的测度，根据 Govindarajan (1988)提出的和公司商业战略相关维度，通过询问应答者相对于主要竞争对手定位来测量公司的战略。这里我们主要从产品成本、研发支出、质量、品牌、服务特色等方面设计了五个问题，问题分值从 1—5。

4. 预算控制紧度

Van der Stede(2001)提出衡量预算控制紧度的五个属性[2]，在我国预算控制紧度的强弱最直接的体现是企业是否将其与员工的考评挂钩，因此我们借鉴了 Van der Stede(2001)从在上司眼中能否实现预算应该是您是否尽职的准确反映、您的提升很大程度上取决于您实现预算的能力、在上司眼中没有实现预算就是业绩差、上司经常提醒您要实现预算等四个方面测度预算的控制紧度。

本文使用卡方/自由度(χ^2/df)、拟合优度指数(GFI)、增值拟合指数(IFI)、调整的拟合优度指数(AGFI)、比较拟合指数(CFI)、近似误差的均方根(RMSEA)来检验模型的拟合程度，并对假设进行检验。

四、实证结果

(一) 描述性统计

收回的有效问卷的描述性统计结果、内部一致性和变量的 Pearson 相关系

[2] Van der Stede(2001)对预算强调和预算调整的定义如下：预算强调包括：(1) 公司高层以我对预算目标的完成情况作为评价我业绩的主要基础；(2) 在我公司上级的眼里，能否实现预算是我能否胜任工作的精确反映；(3) 不能实现预算对我的上级评价我的业绩有重大影响；(4) 我的晋升依赖于我完成预算目标的能力；(5) 在上级的眼中，不能完成预算反映了较差的业绩；(6) 上级经常提醒我完成预算目标的重要性；(7) 母公司主要通过监督子公司完成预算目标的情况控制子公司的经营。预算调整包括：(1) 预算目标是巨大的承诺，不能轻易调整；(2) 预算在一年中经常随着情况的变化而调整；(3) 预算的变更很难得到母公司的同意；(4) 预算随着业务环境的变化按规律地更新；(5) 在本公司，预算实质上是预测而非真实的承诺；(6) 预算在一年中不被修改，除非预算的假设变得不真实以至于不能作为有用的控制工具。注：R 表示反面问题。

数见表 2。Cronbach Alpha 的值一般是介于 0 和 1 之间，越接近于 1，说明信度越高。对于信度系数的最低指标，学者们的要求各不相同，有些学者认为此指标应大于 0.6(Bagozzi and Yi,1988)，有的学者认为大于 0.5 即可(Hair et al.,1998)，也有学者对于个别变量的信度检验采用 0.5 做指标，而对于潜在变量的信度检验要求要高些，采用 0.6 做指标。本文中采用 Bagozzi and Yi(1988)的观点，采用 Alpha 系数大于 0.6 作为衡量量表信度的标准。由表 2 可以看出，除环境不确定性的 Alpha 值为 0.66 外，各变量都有较好的信度，Alpha 值都在 0.7 以上，具有较高的内部一致性。假设变量之间的相关系数都在 0.8 之下，共线性问题不严重。另外，我们发现单变量分析中预算控制紧度和自变量之间的相关系数不显著。

表 2 变量均值、标准差、内部一致性和 Pearson 相关系数

变量	题项数	取值范围	均值	标准差	Alpha	(1)	(2)	(3)
环境不确定性(1)	3	1—5	3.29	0.277	0.66	1		
战略(2)	5	1—5	3.2	0.41	0.72	0.25**	1	
组织分权程度(3)	4	1—5	2.2	0.33	0.82	0.28**	0.14*	1
预算控制紧度(4)	4	1—5	3.03	0.2	0.74	−0.02	0.09	0.11

注：$N=210$，* 在 5% 水平显著，** 在 1% 水平显著。

针对问卷的有效数据，由环境不确定性—战略分量表、组织分权程度分量表以及预算控制紧度分量表的相关矩阵做因子分析的适当性考察，结果见表 3。三个分量表取样适应性的 KMO 检验值分别为 0.72、0.78、0.76，均属可以接受的范围。各分量表 Bartlett 球度检验结果显示测量数据适合对 3 个分量表进行因子分析。

表 3 各分量表 KMO 值和 Bartlett 球度检验

		环境不确定性与战略	组织分权	预算强调
KMO 值		0.72	0.78	0.76
Bartlett's 球度检验	Chi-Square	472**	268.37**	168.93**
	df	28	6	6
	Sig.	0.00	0.00	0.00

注：$N=210$，* 在 5% 水平显著，** 在 1% 水平显著。

（二）验证性因子分析

为了进一步检验量表的结构效度和信度，首先选用 SPSS 11.5 进行信度分析，再对各分量表运用 AMOS 5.0 分别进行验证性因子分析，为结构方程模型分析做铺垫。环境不确定性与战略(自变量)分量表验证性因子分析结果见图

2。其中 PEU 表示环境不确定性，PEU1—PEU3 为环境不确定性的操作变量；CS 表示低成本战略，CS1、CS2 为低成本战略的操作变量；DS 表示差异化战略，DS1—DS3 为差异化战略的操作变量。组织分权程度（中介变量）分量表验证因子分析结果见图 3，其中 DEC 表示组织分权程度，DEC1—DEC4 为组织分权程度操作变量。预算控制紧度（因变量）分量表验证因子分析结果见图 4，其中，BE 表示预算控制紧度，BE1—BE4 为预算控制紧度的操作变量。

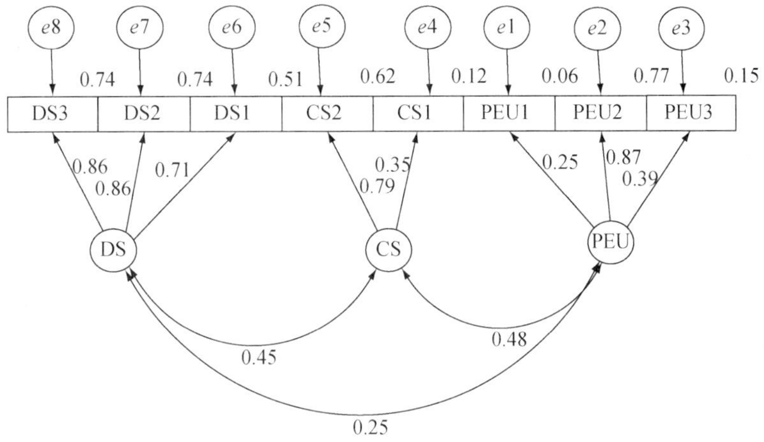

图 2　环境不确定性与战略关系验证因子分析模型

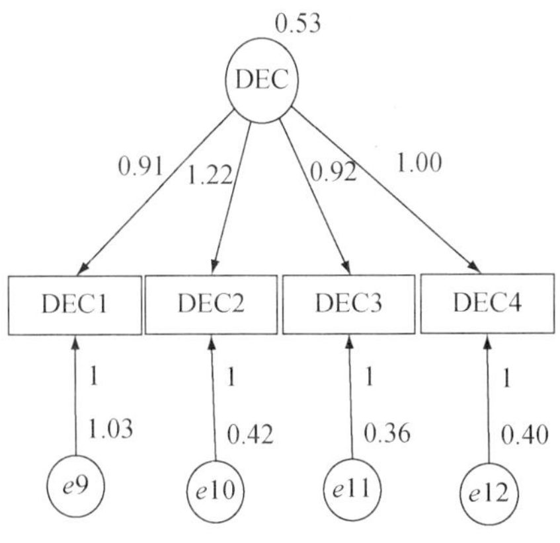

图 3　组织分权程度验证因子分析模型

各分量表的标准化载荷系数见表 4，拟合指数、信度情况见表 5。由表 4 可以看出，对于环境不确定性与战略分量表，2 个因子对操作变量的因子载荷都比较好，且各载荷的 t 值都达到 2.4 以上，即在 5%水平显著。同时，模型的拟合指标 $\frac{\chi^2}{df}=1<2$，$p=0.41>0.05$，GFI＝0.98，AGFI＝0.96，TLI＝0.99，

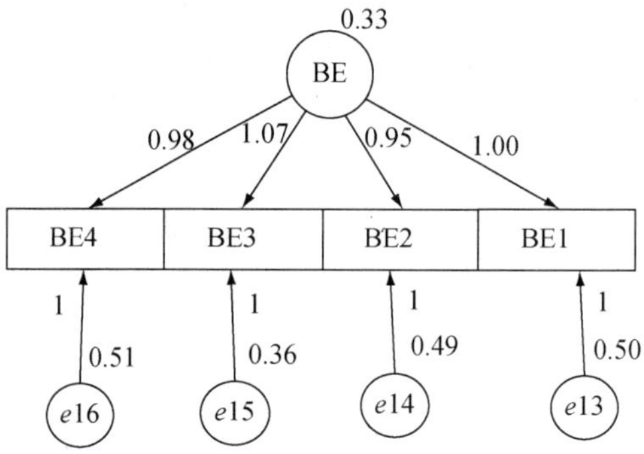

图 4　预算控制紧度验证因子分析模型

CFI＝0.99，都大于 0.9；RMSEA＝0.013，RMR＝0.039，都小于 0.05，所以所有指标都符合模型拟合的基本要求，模型拟合较好。另外，环境不确定性与战略分量表的 Alpha 值为 0.7，符合信度要求。总之，环境不确定性与战略的验证因子分析测量模型的数据具有较高的会聚有效性和判别有效性，效度较好。

表 4　各分量表标准化载荷系数

结构变量	观测变量	标准化载荷系数	*T* 值	信度
环境不确定性(PEU)	PEU1	0.25**	2.4	
	PEU2	0.87		
	PEU3	0.39**	2.9	
成本领先战略(CS)	CS1	0.35**	2.8	
	CS2	0.79		
差异化战略(DS)	DS1	0.71		
	DS2	0.86**	11.0	0.7
	DS3	0.86**	10.9	
组织分权程度(DEC)	DEC1	0.55**	7.2	
	DEC2	0.81**	10.0	
	DEC3	0.74**	9.7	0.8
	DEC4	0.76		
预算控制紧度(BE)	BE1	0.63		
	BE2	0.62**	6.4	
	BE3	0.72**	6.8	0.74
	BE4	0.62**	6.4	

注：*N*＝210，* 在 5％水平显著，** 在 1％水平显著。

表 5　各分量表结构效度和 Alpha 值

分量表名	χ^2	df	p	GFI	AGFI	TLI	CFI	RMSEA	RMR	Alpha
环境不确定性与战略	17.6	17	0.41	0.98	0.96	0.99	0.99	0.013	0.039	0.70
组织分权程度	1.0	2	0.61	0.99	0.99	1.01	1	0	0.010	0.82
预算控制紧度	0.5	2	0.79	0.99	0.99	1.03	1	0	0.007	0.74

注：$N=210$，Chi-Square 为卡方值，df 为自由度，p 为拟合优度的卡方检验值，GFI 为拟合优度指数，AGFI 为调整的拟合优度指数，TLI 为非范拟合指数，CFI 为比较拟合参数，RMSEA 为近似误差均方根，RMR 为残差均方根，Alpha 为信度检验值。

对于组织分权程度分量表，操作变量的因子载荷都比较好，各载荷的 t 值在 7.2 以上，即 0.1%水平显著。同时，模型的拟合指标 $\frac{\chi^2}{df}=0.5<2$，$p=0.61>0.05$，GFI＝0.99，AGFI＝0.99，TLI＝1.01，CFI＝1 都大于 0.9，RMSEA＝0，RMR＝0.01，都小于 0.05，所以所有指标都符合模型拟合的基本要求，模型拟合较好。另外，环境不确定性与战略分量表的 Alpha 值为 0.82，符合信度要求。总之，组织分权程度的验证因子分析测量模型的数据具有较高的会聚有效性和判别有效性，效度较好。

对于预算控制紧度分量表，操作变量的因子载荷都比较好，各载荷的 t 值都 6.4 以上，即 0.1%水平显著。同时，模型的拟合指标 $\frac{\chi^2}{df}=0.25<2$，$p=0.79>0.05$，GFI＝0.99，AGFI＝0.99，TLI＝1.03，CFI＝1 都大于 0.9，RMSEA＝0，RMR＝0.007，都小于 0.05，所以所有指标都符合模型拟合的基本要求，模型拟合较好。另外，环境不确定性与战略分量表的 Alpha 值为 0.74，符合信度要求。总之，预算控制紧度的验证因子分析测量模型的数据具有较高的会聚有效性和判别有效性，效度较好。

（三）假设检验

对结构方程模型进行充分条件和必要条件的识别后，运用 Amos 5.0 统计软件将调查数据与假设路径进行拟合，回归结果见表 6。我们可以看到模型的拟合指标 $\frac{\chi^2}{df}=1.22<2$，$p=0.069>0.05$，GFI＝0.94，AGFI＝0.91，TLI＝0.97，CFI＝0.98，都大于 0.9，RMSEA＝0.03，RMR＝0.048，都小于 0.05，所以所有指标都符合模型拟合的基本要求，模型拟合较好。就回归结果来看，环境不确定性越高预算控制的紧度越低，标准化路径系数为 1.77，统计上 1%水平显著。环境不确定性对组织的分权程度有正面影响，标准化路径系数为0.93，统计上1%水平显著。成本领先战略对预算控制紧度有正面影响，标准化系数为2.24，统计上1%水平显著，差异化战略对预算控制紧度有负面影响，标准化系数为1.12，统计上5%水平显著。成本领先战略对组织的分权程度有负面影响，标准化系数为0.9，统计上5%水平显著；差异化战略对组织的分权程度有正面影响，标准化系数为0.52，统计上5%水平显著。组织分权程度对预算控制紧度有正面影响，标准化系数为0.85，统计上5%水平显著。我们提出的假设都得到了很好的验证。这里我们进一步分析，成本领先战略对预算控制的紧度的总影响最大，达到1.45，环境不确定性对预算控制紧度的总影响为−0.99；差异化战略对预算控制紧度的总影响为−0.67。这也说明成本领先战略下，预算的控制功能的作用更明显。其中，成本领先战略对预算控制紧度的直接影响为2.24，间接影响为−0.76，这说明，随着组织分权程度的提高，成本领先战略下的预算控制紧度下降；环境不确定性对预算控制紧度的直接影响为−1.77，间接影响为0.79，说明外部环境的不确定性增大虽然可以降低预算的控制紧度，但是随着组织分权程度的提高，一定程度上能够适应环境的变化，提高预算的控制紧度；另外，差异化战略对预算控制紧度的直接影响为−1.12，通过组织分权程度对预算控制紧度的间接影响为0.43，这意味着差异化战略需要较松的预算控制，但是组织分权在一定程度上限制了这种趋势，这与Sharma(2002)的研究结果一致。Sharma(2002)对旅馆业的研究表明组织的分权程度与预算的控制和业绩评价功能显著正相关。总之，我们可以看出，组织的分权程度是环境不确定性、战略等因素对于预算控制紧度影响的重要中介变量。

表6 全样本结构方程分析结果

假设路径关系	预测符号	标准化路径系数	*T*值	总影响	直接影响	间接影响	结论
环境不确定性与预算控制紧度(H1)	−	−1.77**	−2.77	−0.99	−1.77	0.79	得到支持
环境不确定性与组织分权程度(H2)	+	0.93**	2.57	0.93	0.93	0	得到支持
成本领先战略与预算控制紧度(H3)	+	2.24**	3.20	1.45	2.24	−0.76	得到支持
差异化战略与预算控制紧度(H4)	−	−1.12*	−2.43	−0.67	−1.12	0.43	得到支持
成本领先战略与组织分权程度(H5)	−	−0.90*	−2.01	−0.90	−0.90	0	得到支持
差异化战略与组织分权程度(H6)	+	0.52*	2.00	0.52	0.52	0	得到支持
组织分权程度与预算控制紧度(H7)	+	0.85*	2.34	0.85	0.85	0	得到支持
χ^2	df	*P*	GFI	AGFI	TLI	CFI	RMSEA	RMR
116	95	0.069	0.94	0.91	0.97	0.98	0.03	0.048

注：*N*=210，* 在5%水平显著，** 在1%水平显著。

五、结论与讨论

我们通过对210份有效问卷进行分析，深入讨论了环境、战略、组织分权程度对预算控制紧度的影响，并且利用结构方程(SEM)验证我们提出的相关假设和影响路径。我们的研究结论是：环境不确定性越高、实施差异化战略的企业的预算控制紧度越低，组织分权程度越高以及实施成本领先战略的企业预算控制紧度越高。我们还发现成本领先战略对预算控制紧度的影响最大，同时，组织分权程度受到环境不确定性、战略的影响，在环境不确定性、战略对预算控制紧度的影响中起着重要的中介作用。

我们的研究验证了Brownell(1985)、Simons(1995)、Govindarajan(1988)以及Sharma(2002)等关于环境不确定性、公司战略以及组织分权程度对预算控制紧度的影响；同时，我们的研究表明，组织分权程度是内生变量，郑石桥(2008)和Zuriekat et al. (2009)等在研究组织结构对预算功能的影响时未考虑其内生性问题，所以其结论高估了组织结构对预算控制紧度的影响。

参考文献

[1] 鲍卫新，2008，任务不确定性对预算控制紧度及控制效果影响之实证研究，《财会月刊(理论)》，第11期，第55—58页。

[2] 蔡剑辉，2009，预算的职能冲突与协调对策研究，《会计研究》，第12期，第55—59页。

[3] 郑石桥等，2008，《预算管理实证研究》，大连：东北财经大学出版社。

[4] Ansoff, I., 1979, *Strategic Management*, New York, John Wiley & Sons.

[5] Anthony and Govindarajan, 1998, *Management Control Systems*, New York, McGraw Hill-Higher Education.

[6] Bagozzi, R. P. and Yi, Y., 1988, On the evaluation of structural equation models, *Journal of the Academy of Marketing Science*, Vol. 16, No. 1, pp. 74—94.

[7] Besanko, D., Dranove, D. and Shanley, M., 1996, *Economics of Strategy*, New York, John Wiley & Sons.

[8] Briers, M. and Hirst, M., 1990, The role of budgetary information in performance evaluation, *Accounting, Organization and Society*, Vol. 15, No. 4, pp. 373—398.

[9] Brownell, P., 1985, Budgetary systems and the control of functionally differentiated organizational activities, *Journal of Accounting Research*, Vol. 23, No. 2, pp. 502—512.

[10] Bruns, W. and Waterhouse, J., 1975, Budgetary control and organization structure, *Journal of Accounting Research*, Vol. 13, No. 2, pp. 177—203.

[11] Chandler, A., 1962, *Strategy and Structure*, Cambridge, MA, M. I. T. Press.

[12] Chenhall, R. H., 2003, Management control systems design within its organizational context: Findings from contingency-based research and directions for the future, *Accounting, Organization and Society*, No. 28, pp. 127—168.

[13] Chenhall, R. H. and Morris, D., 1986, The impact of structure, environment, and interdependence on the perceived usefulness of management accounting systems, *The Accounting Review*, Vol. 61, No. 1, pp. 16—35.

[14] Chia, Y., 1995, Decentralization, management accounting system (MAS) information characteristics and their interaction effects on managerial performance: A Singapore study, *Journal of Business Finance and Accounting*, Vol. 22, No. 6, pp. 811—830.

[15] Child, J., 1972, Organizational structure and strategy of control: A replication of the aston-study, *Administration Science Quarterly*, No. 7, pp. 163—177.

[16] Chow, C. W., Kato, Y. and Merchant, K. A., 1996, The use of organizational controls and-their effects on data manipulation and management myopia: A Japan vs. U. S. comparison, *Accounting, Organizations and Society*, No. 21, pp. 175—192.

[17] Dent, J. F., 1986, *Organizational Research in Accounting: Perspectives, Issues and a Commentary*, London, Pitman.

[18] Dent, J. F., 1990, Strategy, organization and control: Some possibilities for accounting research, *Accounting, Organization and Society*, Vol. 15, No. 1—2, pp. 3—25.

[19] Drucker, P., 1998, Management's new paradigms [EB/OL], http://www.aom-iaom.org/article_drucker.pdf.

[20] Duncan, R. G., 1971, Multiple decision-making structures in adapting to environmental uncertainty: The impact on organizational effectiveness, Working paper, Northwestern University, Graduate School of Management, pp. 54—71.

[21] Fitzgerald, L., Johnston, R. and Brignall, T. J., 1991, *Performance Measurement in Service Business*, London, CIMA.

[22] Gordon, L. A. and Miller, D., 1976, A contingency framework for the design of accounting information systems, *Accounting, Organization and Society*, Vol. 1, No. 1, pp. 59—69.

[23] Gordon, L. A. and Narayanan, V. K., 1984, Management accounting systems, perceived environmental uncertainty and organization structure: An empirical investigation, *Accounting, Organization and Society*, Vol. 9, No. 1, pp. 33—47.

[24] Govindarajan, V., 1984, Appropriateness of accounting data in performance evaluation: An empirical examination of environmental uncertainty as an intervening variable, *Accounting, Organizations and Society*, Vol. 9, pp. 125—135.

[25] Govindarajan, V., 1988, A contingency approach to strategy implementation at The business-unit level: Integrating administrative mechanism with strategy, *Academyof Management Journal*, Vol. 31, No. 4, pp. 828—853.

[26] Hair, J., Anderson, R., Tatham, R. et al., 1998, *Multivariate Data Analysis*, 5th ed. Upper Saddle River, NJ, Prentice Hall.

[27] Hopwood, A. G., 1980, *Organizational and behavioral Aspects of Budgeting and Control*, Oxford, Philip Allan Publishers.

[28] Khandwalla, P. N., 1972, *The Design of Organization*, San Diego, California, Harcourt Brace Jovanovich.

[29] Khandwalla, P. N., 1977, *The Design of Organizations*, Orlando, Florida, Harcourt Brace Jovanovich.

[30] Lawrence, P. and Lorsch, J., 1967, *Organization and Environment: Managing Differentiation and Integration*, Homewood, Illinois, Richard D. Irwin.

[31] Leifer, R. and Huber, G. P., 1978, Relations among perceived environmental uncertainty, organization structure, and boundary-spanning behavior, *Administrative Science Quarterly*, Vol. 22, No. 2, pp. 235—247.

[32] Merchant, K. A., 1981, The design of the corporate budgeting system: Influences on managerial behavior and performance, *The Accounting Review*, Vol. 56, No. 4, pp. 813—829.

[33] Merchant, K. A., 1985a, Organizational controls and discretionary program decision-making, *Accounting, Organizations and Society*, Vol. 10, pp. 67—85.

[34] Merchant, K. A., 1985b, *Control in Business Organizations*, Pitman, Marshfield.

[35] Merchant, K. A., 1990, The effects of financial control on data manipulation and management myopia, *Accounting, Organization and Society*, Vol. 15, No. 4, pp. 291—307.

[36] Miller, D., 1988, Relating Porter's business strategies to environment and structure: Analysis and performance implications, *Academy of Management Journal*, Vol. 31, No. 2, pp. 280—308.

[37] Mintzberg, H., 1979, *The Structuring of Organizations*, Upper Saddle River, NJ, Prentice-Hall.

[38] Otley, D. T., 1980, The contingency theory of management accounting: Achievement and prognosis, *Accounting, Organization and Society*, Vol. 5, No. 4, pp. 413—428.

[39] Otley, D. T., 1978, Budget use and managerial performance, *Journal of Accounting Research*, Vol. 16, No. 1, pp. 122—149.

[40] Ouchi, W. G., 1979, A conceptual framework for the design of organizational control mechanisms, *Management Science*, Vol. 25, No. 9, pp. 833—848.

[41] Porter, M. E., 1980, *Competitive Strategy Techniques for Analyzing Industries and Competitors: With a New Introduction*, New York, Free Press.

[42] Porter, M. E., 1985, *Competitive Advantage*, New York, Free Press.

[43] Ramamurthy, K. , 1990, Role of environmental, organizational and technological factors in information technology implementation in advanced manufacturing: An innovation adoption-diffusion perspective,Pittsburgh, Univ. of Pittsburgh.

[44] Robbins, S. P. , 1990, *Organization Theory*: *Structure*, *Design and Applications*, 3rd, Upper Saddle River, NJ, Prentice Hall.

[45] Samson, D. A. , Langfield-Smith, K. M. and McBride, P. M. , 1991, The alignment of management accounting with manufacturing priorities: A strategic perspective, *The Australian Accounting Review*, Vol. 1, No. 1, pp. 29—40.

[46] Sharma, D. , 2002, The differential effect of environmental dimensionality, size, and structure on budget system characteristics in hotels, *Management Accounting Research*, Vol. 13, pp. 101—130.

[47] Simons, R. , 1987, Accounting control systems and business strategy: An empirical analysis, *Accounting*, *Organization and Society*, Vol. 12, No. 4, pp. 357—374.

[48] Simons, R. , 1990, The role of management control systems in creating competitive advantage: New perspectives, *Accounting*, *Organization and Society*, Vol. 15, No. 1—2, pp. 127—143.

[49] Simons, R. , 1995, *Levers of Control*: *How Managers Use Innovation Control Systems to Drive Strategic Renewal*, Boston, Harvard Business School Press.

[50] Van der Stede, W. A. , 2001, Measure tight budgetary control,*Management Accounting Research*, Vol. 12, No. 1, pp. 119—137.

[51] Van der Stede, W. A. , 2000, The relationship between two consequences of budgetary controls: Budgetary slack creation and managerial short-term orientation, *Accounting*, *Organization and Society*, Vol. 25, No. 6, pp. 609—622.

[52] Waterhouse, J. H. and Tiessen, P. , 1978, A contingency framework for management accounting systems research, *Accounting*, *Organization and Society*, Vol. 3, No. 1, pp. 65—76.

[53] Zuriekat, M. , Khadra, H. A. and Alramahi, N. , 2009,The discrepancy effect of strategy, environment, size and centralization on budgetary characteristics,*Journal of Accounting Business & Management*, Vol. 16, No. 1, pp. 1—21.

The Effect of Perceived Environmental Uncertainty, Strategy and Structure on Budget Tightness: A Survey on Small and Medium-Sized Enterprises of China

LISHENG YU
(*Xiamen University*)
QUAN JIANG
(*Jiangsu Frontier Electric Technology Co. LTD*)

Abstract Based on 210 useable questionnaires, this paper examines the effect of structural decentralization, perceived environmental uncertainty (PEU), and strategy on budget tightness. The results indicate that PEU and differentiation strategy have positive influence on tight budget control, otherwise, structural decentralization and cost leadership strategy have negative influence. The results show that structural decentralization is an important mediating variable.

Key words Budget Tightness, Strategy, Perceived Environmental Uncertainty, Structural Decentralization

管理会计学刊　　JOURNAL OF MANAGEMENT ACCOUNTING STUDIES
第5卷　第1期　　Vol. 5, No. 1

管理者预期对费用粘性的影响研究
——来自中国上市公司的经验数据

王满　曹歌　刘水*

摘　要　本文从管理者预期角度对费用粘性成因进行分析，选取我国沪深两市A股1044家上市公司作为研究样本，发现：(1) 我国上市公司不仅存在费用粘性，也存在费用反粘性；(2) 方向一致的需求预测信号会增强管理者对于未来乐观预期或悲观预期的信心，进而导致费用粘性或反粘性的程度增强，方向不一致的需求预测信号会减少管理者对于未来乐观预期或悲观预期的信心，进而导致费用粘性或反粘性的程度减弱。

关键词　管理者预期，费用粘性，费用反粘性，成本习性

一、引　　言

成本费用粘性[1](cost stickiness)是近年来国内外成本管理领域的研究热点之一(Anderson, Banker and Janakiraman, 2003；孙铮、刘浩，2004；Banker and Chen, 2006；孙玉生、朱乃平、孔庆根，2007；Balakrishnan and Gruca, 2008；Kama and Weiss, 2010；Banker, Ciftci and Mashruwala, 2011；Baumgarten et al. , 2012；陈

* 王满(通信作者)，东北财经大学会计学院，教授、博导，邮编：116025，E-mail：manwang123@163.com；曹歌，中国银行辽宁省分行；刘水，东北财经大学会计学院。该论文为东北财经大学会计学院学术骨干资助项目"构建战略管理会计学科体系研究"的阶段性研究成果。本文选自中国会计学会管理会计分委员会2012年会论文，文章由胡玉明教授接受。

[1] 由于国内外文献对粘性行为的研究对象既包括销售费用，管理费用等期间费用，也包括营业成本，在此本文将其统称为成本费用粘性，并在后文中根据实际情况选用"费用粘性"或"成本粘性"。

磊等,2012 等)。作为一种不对称的成本习性(cost behavior)[2],成本费用粘性具体表现为成本(费用)随业务量增加而上升的幅度大于随业务量等额减少而下降的幅度。由于成本(费用)的跨期变动在很大程度上会受到管理者成本管理决策的影响(Cooper and Kaplan,1998),成本费用粘性的研究实际上是在一定程度上放宽了管理者的理性假设,有利于研究人员通过大样本实证检验的方法揭示成本管理行为这一"黑箱"。

成本费用粘性的形成主要受到三方面因素的影响:首先,受到由于企业内部资源调整而产生的调整成本影响(Anderson, Banker and Janakiraman, 2003);其次,受到由代理问题引发的管理者自利行为的影响(Chen et al.,2008;万寿义、王红军,2011);再次,受到管理者对于未来需求预期的影响(Banker, Ciftci and Mashruwala,2011)。研究人员普遍认为三类成因不是相互独立的,而是互相补充,共同影响着企业成本费用粘性的程度。随着 Banker,Ciftci and Mashruwala(2011)证实了由于管理者预期的不同,美国上市公司不仅存在着费用粘性,也存在着费用反粘性,"管理者预期"成因的研究意义逐步凸显,而我国鲜有"管理者预期与费用粘性"关系的研究。

基于此,本文通过对我国沪深两市 A 股 1044 家上市公司 2008—2011 年度的财务数据进行经验分析,研究中国上市公司的费用是否也存在着反粘性现象,管理者的乐观(悲观)预期是否会导致费用粘性(反粘性)程度的不同,以及其背后的经济意义和理论价值。

二、文献回顾

对于费用粘性成因的研究起始于 Anderson, Banker and Janakiraman (2003)(以下简称 ABJ),ABJ(2003)在最初的研究中已将销管费用粘性的产生原因归结为资源调整成本、代理问题以及管理者乐观预期三大类。ABJ(2003)运用资产强度(assets/sales)及员工强度(employees/sales)作为资源调整成本的替代变量,证实了费用粘性程度会随着资产强度及员工强度的增加而增加,即资源调整成本越高,费用粘性越大。ABJ(2003)认为公司之所以做出保留闲

---

[2] 在 Anderson,Banker and Janakiraman 于 2003 年明确提出"费用粘性"概念之前,成本管理学者将其称为"成本(费用)非对称性"(asymmetric behavior of costs)。

置约束性资源的决策可能是由代理问题产生的管理者自利行为导致的，因为面对市场需求的变动，经理人员既不愿减少自己的薪酬，也不愿削减自己所能控制的资源。除此之外，在ABJ(2003)的研究设计中贯穿着管理者乐观预期的假设，即管理者对于未来需求的判断是乐观的，即使当期销售情况不佳也只是暂时现象，企业业务量的平均趋势是长期增长的，并且通过实证检验证实了管理者乐观预期的程度与费用粘性程度成正比例变动。ABJ(2003)的研究不仅为国内外研究学者提供了验证成本或费用粘性的方法，也为研究成本(费用)粘性的成因提供了基本的分析范式，随后的研究基本上都是在ABJ(2003)研究成果之上的改进和拓展。

在资源调整成本成因的研究中，Subramaniam and Weidenmier (2003)在ABJ(2003)的基础上进一步将样本扩大，并将产业区分为制造业、零售业及服务业，并纳入固定资产强度、员工强度、存货强度及利息费用率，借以检查资源调整成本在不同产业之间存在的差异性。Banker and Chen(2006)以经合组织19个成员国为研究对象，考察了不同国家劳动力市场特征对于企业成本粘性的影响，并发现：公司成本粘性的程度随着这些国家工会的工资谈判权利的增加而增加，随着这些国家劳资谈判中的集权化和协调水平的提高而降低，随着这些国家失业保险金水平的提高而降低，随着这些国家就业保护立法的严格性而增加。Kama and Weiss(2010)认为当未来需求不确定时，企业会更倾向于采取灵活的技术降低资源调整成本，进而降低费用粘性的程度。我国学者龚启辉、刘慧龙和申慧慧(2010)研究发现企业所在地区要素市场发育水平越高，其费用粘性程度越小，进一步为企业所需求资源的调整成本影响企业费用粘性提供了新的证据。

在代理问题成因的研究中，Calleja et al. (2006)比较了美、英、法、德四国企业的销售成本粘性，发现法国和德国企业的成本粘性要强于英美两国，分析其原因，主要是英美的金融体系以资本市场为中心，管理者更加重视股东的利益，而法德的金融体系以银行为中心，管理者更重视利益相关者的利益，这种治理模式的差异导致了法德的公司治理结构要弱于英美。Chen et al. (2008)发现当管理者为了追逐其权力王国而过度投资资源，存在管理者自利的代理问题时，成本费用粘性程度较为严重，而当公司治理结构较好时，成本费用粘性较弱。Kama and Weiss(2010)以美国上市公司为研究对象的实证结果发现，由于管理者具有资源调整的自由裁量权，因此管理者自利行为将影响资源调整的时间、速度和方式，进而影响成本费用粘性。万寿义、王红军(2011)研究发现中国制造业上市公司销管费用粘性行为中存在管理者自利动机和机会主义因素，销管费用粘性随着公司自由现金持有量的增加而增加。

上述两类成因的分析范式在近年来国内外的研究中不断地丰富和发展，其研究设计基本以ABJ(2003)模式为基础，即在不改变其对管理者乐观预期这一前提的基础上展开。然而，近年来对于费用粘性存在性的质疑却为研究人员拓展了其他的研究路径。Anderson and Lanen(2007)以及Dierynek and Renders(2009)等在其研究中陆续发现了成本(费用)反粘性，陈磊、宋乐、施丹(2012)在其研究中也发现了我国上市公司费用粘性存在高估的嫌疑。Banker, Ciftci and Mashruwala(2011)则从影响费用粘性的管理者预期成因入手，改造了ABJ(2003)的研究思路，将管理者的预期分为乐观与悲观两种情形，并经研究发现，乐观的管理者在销售量上升时更愿意增加生产能力，会产生销管费用粘性；而悲观的管理者在销售量下降时更愿意减少生产能力，会产生销管费用反粘性。该研究实际上是拓宽了ABJ(2003)对于管理者乐观预期的研究视角，加入了更为短期的因素，从而使研究模型更符合当今企业管理环境日新月异的变化，其结论也更为准确。目前我国的研究基本上沿用了ABJ(2003)的分析模式，假设管理者对未来的预期是乐观的，尚未加入短期变化的因素。因此，“我国的销管费用是否也存在反粘性”、“我国管理者乐观(悲观)预期对于费用粘性(反粘性)的影响程度如何”都是值得我国研究者进一步探索的问题。

三、研究假设

(一) 管理者预期和费用粘性或反粘性的相关性

在现有的会计研究文献当中，资源产能规划决策已经被广泛地研究。当管理者对于是否以及如何调整资源产能做决策时，他们必须首先考虑现有资源的产能和未来对资源产能的需求(Banker, Hwang and Mishra, 2002)。基于上述评估，管理者必须在以下两者中进行权衡：获得过多的产能导致产能剩余成本，获得过少的产能导致销售损失。这就需要管理者根据当前和过去的经济形势以及公司的需求趋势来预测未来需求的增长情况。管理者对于未来需求情况过于乐观，将导致他们增加更多的生产能力；相反，当管理者对未来需求悲观时，他们会更愿意削减产能。

本文考虑到了ABJ(2003)研究框架中前期销售变化的重要性。在我国的会计制度背景下，研究者多采用“营业收入”来表示销售的变化趋势。首先，我们考虑了基于前期（$t-1$ 期）营业收入增长的情况，考虑到营业收入在前期的增长管理者判断需求是增加的，很可能产生乐观心理。如果营业收入在当期（t 期）再次增长，将会导致管理者对未来销售更强烈的乐观预期，从而使管理者更愿意增加资源产能；但是如果营业收入在第 t 期减少，管理者会由于前期营业收入增长、减少的交替变化和对未来需求的不确定而不太乐意削减资源。接下来，本文考虑了当营业收入在 $t-1$ 期减少时费用的变化。考虑到营业收入在前期的减少，管理者更可能是悲观的。如果营业收入在 t 期增长，管理者会由于营业收入变化的冲突信号而对增加产能资源的策略不那么乐观，但是如果营业收入在 t 期下降，则会增加管理者对于未来需求的悲观预期，并且因此更愿意在未来期间削减产能，这会导致反粘性成本习性。因此，本文预期依照前期营业收入变化导致的两种截然相反却共存的过程——当营业收入在前期增长时导致当期费用粘性的乐观过程；当前期营业收入下降时导致费用反粘性的悲观过程。通过对现有 ABJ 模型的分析，笔者注意到，基于同期销售变化的单期模型不能够区分这两个平行的过程。因此，这两种效应在所有样本中被淘汰，并且平均值的获得是由样本是否由销售下降或上升观察值的相对数填充。

本文在假设 1a 与假设 1b 中，检验由未来需求判断所获得的管理者乐观与悲观预期引起的费用粘性与反粘性，具体如下：

假设 1a 当前期营业收入增长时（乐观预期过程），当期销管费用呈现出粘性（费用随着销售增长而上扬的幅度大于随着销售减少而下降的幅度）。

假设 1b 当前期营业收入减少时（悲观预期过程），当期销管费用呈现出反粘性（费用随着销售减少而下降的幅度大于随着销售增长而上扬的幅度）。

（二）方向一致的需求预测信号对费用粘性或反粘性的影响

本文的研究思路是用前期销售情况替代未来需求判断，形成管理者的乐观预期与悲观预期，进而探讨管理者预期对于费用粘性的影响。笔者认为 ABJ 模型基于前期销售变化的条件下，会导致相关的费用粘性或反粘性的出现。基于相似的推理，本文预期在连续前两期销售收入增长的子样本中发现最具粘性的成本习性，因为这种情形代表了最大的管理者乐观预期。同时，拓展悲观的情形，我们期待最严重的反成本粘性将会出现在前两期销售收入连续减少的子样本中，因为这种情形代表了最大的管理者悲观预期。我们将假设阐释如下：

假设 2a　在前两期营业收入增加的情况下，当期的销管费用呈现最强的粘性；

假设 2b　在前两期营业收入减少的情况下，当期的销管费用呈现最强的反粘性。

当考虑多重信号时，就会产生一个问题：如果不同的信号彼此冲突怎么办？行为经济学中的确认理论（Rabin and Schrag，1999）认为如果大多数信号在同方向上是一致的，管理者会更愿意将注意力集中于彼此一致的信号，进而形成他们的愿景，忽略那些与愿景冲突的信号。本文依照行为理论中管理者对于冲突和一致信号的反映，预测管理者将如何在制定决策的过程中管理资源整合这些信号。本文基于销售变化在当期与前两期的方向，观察三期模型，考虑管理者乐观预期与悲观预期来检测这个问题。在这种情况下，我们可以根据营业收入变化在考虑三阶段的情况下得到 8 种情形。例如，在 $I_tI_{t-1}D_{t-1}$ 的情形下，营业收入将会在 t 期与 $t-1$ 期上升，但是 $t-2$ 期下降，等等。为了便于整合结果，我们将这些情形分为三组：组 1 是最一致的，销售变化在三期变化的方向是相同的（也就是说，$I_tI_{t-1}I_{t-2}$ 与 $D_tD_{t-1}D_{t-2}$）；组 2 是在近两期的销售变化是一致的（即，$I_tI_{t-1}D_{t-2}$ 与 $D_tD_{t-1}I_{t-2}$）；组 3 是在近两期不一致，$t-1$ 期与 t 期销售变化的方向不同（即 $I_tD_{t-1}D_{t-2}$，$D_tI_{t-1}I_{t-2}$，$I_tD_{t-1}I_{t-2}$ 与 $D_tI_{t-1}D_{t-2}$）。

基于行为经济学理论，我们预期成本变化在组 1 中最大，这一观点与 Johnson-Laird et al.（1999）的研究结果一致。当管理者观察三期的营业收入变化是同方向的，由于观察信号是彼此佐证的，他们将会对营业收入在下期变化的预期更有信心。换言之，对于组 1 中的情形，他们会极度的乐观（$I_tI_{t-1}I_{t-2}$）和极度的悲观（$D_tD_{t-1}D_{t-2}$），结果他们将会更愿意去调整产能。对于组 3 中的情形而言，一方面，近两期（t 期与 $t-1$ 期）的信号是彼此冲突的，这种冲突将会导致管理者对于未来的需求情况产生更强烈的不确定性，最终管理者对于未来需求方向判断的信心将会低于组 2。因此，对于组 2 中的情形，当销售在当期增长时（$I_tI_{t-1}D_{t-2}$），管理者将会更加乐观，当销售在当期减少时（$D_tD_{t-1}I_{t-2}$），管理者将会更加悲观。另一方面，他们将会因为销售信号在最近的两个时期相反，而对未来需求持中立态度。因此，与组 3 相比，处于组 2 中的管理者将更愿意做出产能调整。根据以上论述，我们预期如下：

假设 2c　组 1 中销管费用随着营业收入变化的相对幅度大于组 2 与组 3。

假设 2d　组 2 中销管费用随着营业收入变化的相对幅度大于组 3。

四、研究设计

（一）模型设计

ABJ(2003)采用对数线性模型对费用粘性进行检测，随后的研究人员以这一模型为蓝本添加控制变量和解释因素，ABJ 模型[3]具体如下：

$$\Delta SG\&A_{i,t} = \beta_0 + \beta_1 \times \Delta REV_{i,t} + \beta_2 \times D_{i,t} \times \Delta REV_{i,t} + \varepsilon_{i,t} \quad (1)$$

虽然这一模型被广泛地运用于解释费用粘性的成因，但是也存在着如下局限性：一是没有区分销售上升或下降的情况，存在高估费用粘性、忽略费用反粘性存在的可能(Anderson and Lanen, 2007)；二是无法全面地反映管理者预期对费用粘性的影响，只是假定管理者永远乐观，忽视了管理者悲观预期可能对费用粘性产生的影响(Banker et al.，2011)。因此，本文参考了 Banker et al.(2011)的做法，对上述 ABJ 模型进行了拓展，重新构筑费用粘性与反粘性的分析范式，从而更有效地证明管理者预期对于费用粘性的影响。

1. 两期模型

为了验证假设中的“管理者乐观预期—费用粘性”和“管理者悲观预期—费用反粘性”，本文继续运用对数线性模型[4]，对 ABJ 模型进行拓展，以便能在两个公司的子样本(营业收入增长；营业收入下降)中同时检测出费用的不对称性。本文用以下反映前期与当期营业收入变化的模型检测假设 1a 与假设 1b，模型中变量的界定详见表 1：

$$\Delta SG\&A_{i,t} = \beta_0 + \beta_1^{OPT} \times I_{i,t-1} \times \Delta REV_{i,t} + \beta_2^{OPT} \times D_{i,t} I_{i,t-1} \times \Delta REV_{i,t} + \beta_1^{PES} \times D_{i,t-1} \times \Delta REV_{i,t} + \beta_2^{PES} \times D_{i,t} D_{i,t-1} \times \Delta REV_{i,t} + \varepsilon_{i,t} \quad (2)$$

模型 2 相当于整合了两个 ABJ 模型(1)于一个相同的等式之中[5]，在假设 1a 的基础(前期营业收入 $I_{i,t-1}$ 增加)上，虚拟变量 $D_{i,t}I_{i,t-1}$ 在本期营业收入减少时

---

[3] 其中，$\Delta SG\&A_{i,t}$ 是 i 公司在 t 年销售管理费用相对于第 $t-1$ 年变化的自然对数；$\Delta REV_{i,t}$ 是 i 公司在 t 年营业收入相对于第 $t-1$ 年变化的自然对数。$D_{i,t}$ 是虚拟变量，在 t 期销售下降时取值 1。

[4] 承继 ABJ 的研究，我们基于三点考虑运用对数线性模型。首先，本文运用了 Davidson and MacKinnon (1981)测试去检测对数线性模型相对于线性模型的适用性。考虑到对数线性模型的优势，线性模型被淘汰。其次，横截面与综合估计值很可能造成异方差。对数线性模型减少了潜在的估计中的异方差。再次，使用对数线性模型有助于对系数的经济学解释。

[5] 检测两个独立子样本的 ABJ 模型应当需要两个不同的截距项。但是本文的研究重点是联系成本变化与销售变化之间的斜率系数而不是截距项。因此，本研究的模型只包括一个截距项。我们通过增加一个额外的截距项来检测所有模型结果的稳定性。在所有情况下的结果具有相似的属性。

为 1，增加时为 0。因此，β_1^{OPT} 度量了当期销管费用对营业收入增加的变化，即营业收入增加 1%，销管费用增加 β_1^{OPT}%，$\beta_1^{OPT}+\beta_2^{OPT}$ 度量了当期销售费用对营业收入减少的变化，即营业收入减少 1%，费用粘性降低（$\beta_1^{OPT}+\beta_2^{OPT}$）%，此时，如果费用粘性存在粘性行为，则有 $\beta_1^{OPT}>\beta_1^{OPT}+\beta_2^{OPT}$，即 $\beta_2^{OPT}<0$。同理，依照本文对费用反粘性的定义，在假设 1b 的基础上，$\beta_2^{PES}>0$。

2. 三阶段模型

在考虑 t 期、$t-1$ 期、$t-2$ 期销售收入变化的基础上，本文对模型(2)进行拓展，形成三阶段模型来检验假设 2a 和假设 2b：

$$\begin{aligned}\Delta SG\&A_{i,t}=&\beta_0+\beta_1^{II}\times I_{t-1}I_{t-2}\times\Delta REV_{i,t}+\beta_2^{II}\times D_tI_{t-1}I_{t-2}\times\Delta REV_{i,t}\\&+\beta_1^{ID}\times I_{t-1}D_{t-2}\times\Delta REV_{i,t}+\beta_2^{ID}\times D_tI_{t-1}D_{t-2}\times\Delta REV_{i,t}\\&+\beta_1^{DI}\times D_{t-1}I_{t-2}\times\Delta REV_{i,t}+\beta_2^{DI}\times D_tD_{t-1}I_{t-2}\times\Delta REV_{i,t}\\&+\beta_1^{DD}\times D_{t-1}D_{t-2}\times\Delta REV_{i,t}+\beta_2^{DD}\times D_tD_{t-1}D_{t-2}\times\Delta REV_{i,t}\\&+\varepsilon_t\end{aligned}\tag{3}$$

与模型(2)的经济意义相似，模型(3)中的系数 β_1^{II} 和 β_2^{II} 代表了在前两期营业收入连续增长的条件下销管费用的变化。对于系数 β_2^{II} 的检测将会揭露在 $t-1$ 期与 $t-2$ 期营业收入增长时，销管费用随着营业收入线性变化的不同，如果 $\beta_2^{II}<0$ 代表着费用呈现粘性，如果 $\beta_2^{II}>0$ 说明费用呈现反粘性。类似的推理可以运用到系数 β_2^{ID}、β_2^{DI} 和 β_2^{DD}，其中上标表示营业收入在前两期的方向变化（也就是说，对于 $t-1$ 期与 $t-2$ 期，I 代表上升，D 代表下降）。

如果将本文的理性推理由两期拓展到三期，本文预测最具粘性的情况是销售收入连续两期上升（$I_{t-1}I_{t-2}$）。在 $I_{t-1}D_{t-2}$ 的情况下，由于前一期的销售收入是增长的，成本将仍然保持粘性，但是程度低于 $I_{t-1}I_{t-2}$。在 $D_{t-1}I_{t-2}$ 的情况下，由于前一期销售收入的下降，本文预期成本会呈现反粘性。最后，在 $D_{t-1}D_{t-2}$ 的情况下，我们预计会看到在 $t-1$ 期、$t-2$ 期销售收入下降的情况下出现最具反粘性的成本习性。

本文通过三阶段假设推演中所描述的 8 种情形，构建出能够检验假设 2c 与假设 2d 的三阶段模型：

$$\begin{aligned}\Delta SG\&A_{i,t}=&\beta_0+\beta_1\times I_tI_{t-1}I_{t-2}\times\Delta REV_{i,t}+\beta_2\times D_tD_{t-1}D_{t-2}\times\Delta REV_{i,t}\\&+\beta_3\times I_tI_{t-1}D_{t-2}\times\Delta REV_{i,t}+\beta_4\times D_tD_{t-1}I_{t-2}\times\Delta REV_{i,t}\\&+\beta_5\times I_tD_{t-1}D_{t-2}\times\Delta REV_{i,t}+\beta_6\times D_tI_{t-1}I_{t-2}\times\Delta REV_{i,t}\\&+\beta_7\times I_tD_{t-1}I_{t-2}\times\Delta REV_{i,t}+\beta_8\times D_tI_{t-1}D_{t-2}\times\Delta REV_{i,t}\\&+\varepsilon_t\end{aligned}\tag{4}$$

在此模型中，当营业收入在第 t 期到 $t-2$ 期这三段期间都上升（下降），虚

拟变量 $I_tI_{t-1}I_{t-2}$($D_tD_{t-1}D_{t-2}$)取值为1,否则为0;如果销售收入在 t 期与 $t-1$ 期增加(下降)但是在 $t-2$ 期减少(增加),虚拟变量 $I_tI_{t-1}D_{t-2}$($D_tD_{t-1}I_{t-2}$)取值为1,否则取值为0;如果销售收入在 t 期减少(增加),在 $t-1$ 期增加(减少),在 $t-2$ 期减少(增加),虚拟变量 $D_tI_{t-1}D_{t-2}$($I_tD_{t-1}I_{t-2}$)取值为1,否则取值为0。

根据假设2c,我们预期当管理者对未来需求高度自信时(如组1),费用的变化将会强于当他们在不太自信的情况(组2或组3)。因此,费用在组1中的变化幅度将会大于组2与组3。假设2d预期费用在组2中的变化幅度将会大于组3,这是因为管理者在组2的情形下会对销售变化更有信心(也就是当期销售收入增加时管理者更乐观,当期销售收入减少时管理者更悲观)。

本文研究变量的选取和定义如表1所示。

表1 变量定义表

变量	变量代码	变量定义
被解释变量	$\Delta SG\&A_{i,t}$	第 i 家公司第 t 期的销售管理费用与第 $t-1$ 期销售管理费用之比的自然对数
解释变量	$\Delta REV_{i,t}$	第 i 家公司第 t 期的营业收入与第 $t-1$ 期营业收入之比的自然对数
	$I_{i,t-1}$	虚拟变量,当第 i 家公司第 $t-1$ 期的营业收入大于第 $t-2$ 期的营业收入时,取1,否则取0
	$D_{i,t-1}$	虚拟变量,当第 i 家公司第 $t-1$ 期营业收入小于第 $t-2$ 期营业收入时,取1,否则取0
	$D_{i,t}I_{i,t-1}$	虚拟变量,当第 i 家公司营业收入在 t 期减少,$t-1$ 期增加时,取1,否则取0
	$D_{i,t}D_{i,t-1}$	虚拟变量,当第 i 家公司营业收入在 $t-1$ 期、t 期连续减少时,取1,否则取0
	$I_tI_{t-1}I_{t-2}$	虚拟变量,当第 i 家公司营业收入在 $t-2$ 期、$t-1$ 期、t 期连续增加时,取1,否则取0
	$D_tD_{t-1}D_{t-2}$	虚拟变量,当第 i 家公司营业收入在 $t-2$ 期、$t-1$ 期、t 期连续减少时,取1,否则取0
	$D_tD_{t-1}I_{t-2}$	虚拟变量,当第 i 家公司营业收入在 $t-2$ 期增加,在 $t-1$ 期、t 期减少时,取1,否则取0
	$D_tI_{t-1}I_{t-2}$	虚拟变量,当第 i 家公司营业收入在 $t-2$ 期、$t-1$ 期增加,在 t 期减少时,取1,否则取0
	$I_tI_{t-1}D_{t-2}$	虚拟变量,当第 i 家公司营业收入在 $t-2$ 期减少,在 $t-1$ 期、t 期增加时,取1,否则取0
	$I_tD_{t-1}D_{t-2}$	虚拟变量,当第 i 家公司营业收入在 $t-2$ 期、$t-1$ 期减少,在 t 期增加时,取1,否则取0
	$I_tD_{t-1}I_{t-2}$	虚拟变量,当第 i 家公司营业收入在 $t-2$ 期增加、$t-1$ 期减少、t 期增加时,取1,否则取0
	$D_tI_{t-1}D_{t-2}$	虚拟变量,当第 i 家公司营业收入在 $t-2$ 期减少、$t-1$ 期增加、t 期减少时,取1,否则取0

（二）样本选择与数据来源

由于我国于2007年开始实施新会计准则，与旧准则在会计核算上存在重大差异，同时，考虑到本文模型中运用了上一年度的营业收入和销管费用作为基期数据，本文将2008—2011年定位为样本选择区间。本文选取沪深两市A股上市公司2008—2011年度财务数据进行经验研究，数据来源于国泰君安研究服务中心的"CSMAR中国上市公司财务报表数据库"。本文按照如下标准对公司样本进行了筛选：(1)剔除了金融保险类上市公司，因为财务报表和管制性质和其他类型公司相比具有特殊性；(2)剔除被ST或PT的上市公司；(3)剔除以前年度营业收入连续观测值不足3年、费用观测值不足1年的上市公司；(4)剔除其他变量的缺失值；(5)剔除营业收入或销售费用或管理费用不大于0的公司；(6)营业收入大于销管费用的公司。共得到1044家上市公司的4 176个年度观测值，具体行业分布如表2。从表2可以看出，样本的行业分布并不是均衡的，1 044家上市公司中，有57.66%是制造类企业，其次为房地产业，占比为8.72%，分布最少的是传播与文化产业，仅为1.05%。

表2 样本公司行业分布

行业类型	样本公司数(家)	所占比重
农、林、牧、渔业	20	1.92%
采掘业	28	2.68%
制造业	602	57.66%
电力、煤气及水的生产和供应业	40	3.83%
建筑业	18	1.72%
交通运输、仓储业	29	2.78%
信息技术业	52	4.98%
批发和零售贸易	90	8.62%
房地产业	91	8.72%
社会服务业	28	2.68%
传播与文化产业	11	1.05%
综合类	35	3.35%
总计	1044	100.00%

五、实证结果分析

（一）描述性统计

表 3 为本研究中变量的描述性统计结果。

表 3 变量描述性统计结果

	均值	中位数	最大值	最小值	标准差
营业收入（万元）	787 925.58	181 943.67	250 568 300.00	1 331.13	5 982 078.97
销管费用（万元）	64 507.22	19 616.59	10 148 200.00	752.89	315 825.47
营业收入变化率	32.23%	14.10%	14 024.14%	−98.43%	261.39%
销管费用变化率	23.93%	14.50%	2 743.77%	−83.73%	89.45%
费用收入比	13.98%	11.26%	97.07%	0.41%	10.93%

营业收入变化率的平均值为 32.23%、中位数是 14.10%，说明 2008—2011 年 1044 家上市公司的 4 176 个观测值（firm-years）总体呈现上升趋势；最大值和最小值分别为 14 024.14%和−98.43%，标准差高达 261.39%，说明样本观测值的差异较大。销管费用变化率的平均值为 23.93%、中位数为 14.50%，说明样本公司的销管费用在样本区间内总体上是增长的；最大值和最小值依次为 2 743.77%和−83.73%，标准差为 89.45%，说明样本公司的销管费用变动情况较大。从整体的描述性统计可以看出，营业收入和销管费用的变化波动较大，为进一步观察样本观测值的变化情况，进而研究管理者预期对费用粘性的影响，本文根据当期（t 期）和前期（$t-1$ 期）营业收入增长或下降的情况对样本观测值进行了划分，具体如表 4 所示。

表 4 观测值分布

$t-1$ 期 \ t 期	营业收入增加	营业收入减少	比重
营业收入增加	45.76%	22.84%	68.61%
营业收入减少	22.80%	8.60%	31.39%
比重	68.56%	31.44%	100%

从表 4 可以看出，$t-1$ 期与 t 期营业收入均有增长的公司占总观测值的比重为 45.76%，占主导；t 期与 $t-1$ 期增长方向不一致的公司占比 45.64%（22.84%+22.80%），与营业收入连续两期增加的公司所占的比重相当；而营

业收入连续两期减少的公司仅占8.6%。在理论分析中，本文推导出以t—1期营业收入的变化判断t期管理者对于需求的预期状况，可以看出，乐观预期(t—1期营业收入增长)和悲观预期(t—1期营业收入减少)下的公司比重分别为68.61%和31.96%，说明在本文样本2008—2011年中，大部分管理者对于未来需求判断更倾向于乐观的预期。

（二）回归结果与分析

1. 费用粘性两期模型回归结果

表5中显示了模型(2)的回归结果，系数均显示了预期的方向。系数β_1^{OPT}为0.556，(p值小于0.01)，而系数β_2^{OPT}的估计值为-0.099(p值小于0.01)。因此，对于营业收入在t—1期增加的公司子样本，费用随着营业收入增加而上扬的幅度高于随着营业收入减少而下降的幅度，但是粘性程度发生了较大的缩水，仅为9.9%，这与以往运用ABJ(2003)进行计算的粘性程度有较大差异。

表5　费用粘性两期模型回归结果

变量	预期符号	模型(2)
Constant(β_0)		0.083*** (20.420)
$I_{i,t-1}\times\Delta REV_{i,t}(\beta_1^{OPT})$	+	0.556*** (33.000)
$D_{i,t}I_{i,t-1}\times\Delta REV_{i,t}(\beta_2^{OPT})$	—	−0.099*** (−4.310)
$D_{i,t-1}\times\Delta REV_{i,t}(\beta_1^{PES})$	+	0.329*** (18.272)
$D_{i,t}D_{i,t-1}\times\Delta REV_{i,t}(\beta_2^{PES})$	+	0.091*** (2.929)
Durbin-Watson	1.965	
Adj-R^2	0.366	
F值	602.966***	
N值	4 176	

注：在本表中，***、**、*分别表示在1%、5%和10%的水平上显著。

系数β_2^{PES}的估计值为0.091，取正值而且显著，说明当前期营业收入下降时，销管费用呈反粘性，即销管费用随着营业收入减少而下降的幅度要大于随着相同数量营业收入增加而上升的幅度。因此，考虑到前一期的销售下降，出现了与ABJ(2003)研究相反的结果。这些结果为本文的假设1a和假设1b提供了证据，在给定的公司样本中，粘性与反粘性两种成本习性并存着——一般而言，当前期销售增加时，费用呈粘性；当前期销售减少时，费用呈反粘性。以往研究费用粘性的单期模型忽略了前期销售变化，因此不能区分这两个过程。而国内外学者运用 ABJ 模型验证费用粘性的存在具有普遍性，很可能是因为样本主要由前期（$t-1$ 期）营业收入增长的观测值组成（如表 3 中所示，对于 $t-1$ 期营业收入的公司观测值中，营业收入增长占 68.61%，但是营业收入下降仅占 31.39%。）

2. 费用粘性三期模型回归结果

表 6 中显示了模型(3)的回归结果，系数均显示了预期的方向。其中，系数 β_2^{II} 的估计值为 -0.169（p 值小于 0.01），说明在前两期（$t-1$ 期、$t-2$ 期）营业收入增加的情况下，销管费用呈现粘性。系数 β_2^{ID} 符号与预期一致，但是结果不显著，说明营业收入在 $t-1$ 期增加、$t-2$ 期减少的情况下，受到需求冲突信号的干扰，管理者对于未来需求情况的乐观预期变弱，进而导致了费用粘性不明显。因此，对于费用粘性的三期回归模型而言，在前两期营业收入增加的情况

表 6 费用粘性三期模型回归结果

变量	预期符号	模型(3)
Constant(β_0)		0.082*** (19.975)
$I_{t-1}I_{t-2}\times\Delta REV_{i,t}(\beta_1^{II})$	+	0.598*** (25.971)
$D_tI_{t-1}I_{t-2}\times\Delta REV_{i,t}(\beta_2^{II})$	−	−0.169*** (−5.368)
$I_{t-1}D_{t-2}\times\Delta REV_{i,t}(\beta_1^{ID})$	+	0.515*** (22.645)
$D_tI_{t-1}D_{t-2}\times\Delta REV_{i,t}(\beta_2^{ID})$	−	−0.025 (−0.756)
$D_{t-1}I_{t-2}\times\Delta REV_{i,t}(\beta_1^{DI})$	+	0.334*** (14.452)
$D_tD_{t-1}I_{t-2}\times\Delta REV_{i,t}(\beta_2^{DI})$	+	0.024 (0.653)
$D_{t-1}D_{t-2}\times\Delta REV_{i,t}(\beta_1^{DD})$	+	0.324*** (11.760)
$D_tD_{t-1}D_{t-2}\times\Delta REV_{i,t}(\beta_2^{DD})$	+	0.259*** (4.696)
Durbin-Watson	1.966	
Adj-R^2	0.369	
F 值	306.547***	
N 值	4 176	

注：在本表中，***、**、* 分别表示在 1%、5%和 10%的水平上显著。

下，当期的销管费用呈现最强的粘性，为假设 2a 提供了证明。系数 β_2^{DD} 估计值为 0.259（p 值小于 0.01），说明在前两期（$t-1$ 期、$t-2$ 期）营业收入减少的情况下，销管费用呈现反粘性。系数 β_2^{ID} 符号与预期一致，但是结果不显著，说明营业收入在 $t-1$ 期减少、$t-2$ 期增加的情况下，受到未来需求判断的冲突信号的干扰，管理者对于未来需求情况的悲观预期变弱，进而导致了费用反粘性不明显。因此，对于费用粘性的三期回归模型而言，在前两期营业收入减少的情况下，当期的销管费用呈现最强的反粘性，为假设 2b 提供了证明。

为了验证假设 2c 与假设 2d，本文对模型（4）进行了回归，结果如表 7 所示。系数方向均与预期一致，且均显著。根据假设 2c 与假设 2d 中的推演，系数按照三期营业收入变化方向分为 8 种情形，β_1—β_8 代表销管费用随着营业收入变化的相对幅度，模型（4）的回归结果重点在于比较不同情况下系数的大小。其中，系数 β_1 的估计值是 0.598（p 值小于 0.01），系数 β_2 的估计值是 0.584（p 值小于 0.01），分别代表着管理者乐观预期下费用粘性最强的情形和管理者悲观预

表 7　费用粘性三期模型回归结果

变量	预期符号	模型(4)
Constant(β_0)		0.082*** (19.975)
$I_t I_{t-1} I_{t-2} \times \Delta REV_{i,t}(\beta_1)$	+	0.598*** (25.971)
$D_t D_{t-1} D_{t-2} \times \Delta REV_{i,t}(\beta_2)$	+	0.584*** (12.217)
$I_t I_{t-1} D_{t-2} \times \Delta REV_{i,t}(\beta_3)$	+	0.515*** (22.645)
$D_t D_{t-1} I_{t-2} \times \Delta REV_{i,t}(\beta_4)$	+	0.491*** (20.885)
$I_t D_{t-1} D_{t-2} \times \Delta REV_{i,t}(\beta_5)$	+	0.324*** (11.760)
$D_t I_{t-1} I_{t-2} \times \Delta REV_{i,t}(\beta_6)$	+	0.429*** (20.086)
$I_t D_{t-1} I_{t-2} \times \Delta REV_{i,t}(\beta_7)$	+	0.334*** (14.452)
$D_t I_{t-1} D_{t-2} \times \Delta REV(\beta_8)$	+	0.359*** (12.318)
Durbin-Watson	1.966	
Adj-R^2	0.369	
F 值	306.547	
N 值	4176	

期下费用反粘性最强的情形，这说明在组1（即$I_tI_{t-1}I_{t-2}$和$D_tD_{t-1}D_{t-2}$）中，销管费用随着营业收入变化的相对幅度最大，这与假设2c一致，预示着如果管理者连续得到了方向相同的需求预期信号，将会增加他们对于未来需求情况的乐观预期或悲观预期的信心。组2（即$I_tI_{t-1}D_{t-2}$和$D_tD_{t-1}I_{t-2}$）中销管费用的变化的相对幅度分别为0.515（β_3）和0.491（β_4）。组3（$I_tD_{t-1}D_{t-2}$，$D_tI_{t-1}I_{t-2}$，$I_tD_{t-1}I_{t-2}$和$D_tI_{t-1}D_{t-2}$）中销管费用变化的相对幅度分别为0.324（β_5）、0.429（β_6）、0.334（β_7）和0.359（β_8）。因此，回归结果显示组2中销管费用变化对于营业收入变化的相对幅度小于组1中的两种情形，却大于组3中的四种情形。这说明当管理者收到近两期营业收入变化的连续一致的信号时，他们对于未来需求或乐观或悲观的判断信心会大于收到近两期营业收入不一致的冲突信号时的信心，这与假设2d相一致。

六、研究结论与建议

管理者预期作为费用粘性的主要成因，一直是国内外研究者重视的问题，但是其主观色彩较重，在有限理性的范围内研究，变量的选取、理论的剖析均具有一定的难度和复杂性，这也制约了对这一成因研究的理论深度和实证可行度。本文采用国外最近研究成果Banker et al.（2011），运用我国上市公司年报数据对这一领域进行探索，得到了如下结论：

（1）我国上市公司不仅存在费用粘性，也存在费用反粘性。本文将样本分为两类：前期营业收入增长和前期营业收入下降。在此基础上，构筑了“前期营业收入增加——管理者乐观预期——费用粘性”和“前期营业收入减少——管理者悲观预期——费用反粘性”两条并存的研究路径。基于这种思路，当我国上市公司前期营业收入增长时，本期营业收入增加1%，销管费用增加0.556%，本期营业收入减少1%，销管费用减少0.457%，存在费用粘性；当我国上市公司前期营业收入减少时，本期营业收入增加1%，销管费用增加0.329%，本期营业收入减少1%，销管费用减少0.42%，存在费用反粘性。

（2）方向一致的需求预测信号会增强管理者对于未来乐观预期或悲观预期的信心，进而导致费用粘性或反粘性的程度增强；方向不一致的需求预测信号会减少管理者对于未来乐观预期或悲观预期的信心，进而导致费用粘性或反粘性的程度减弱。在本文的三期研究模型中，当t期、$t-1$期、$t-2$期营业收入连续增加或连续减少时，费用粘性或反粘性的程度显著，当三期营业收入出现交替增加减少、趋势不统一时，费用粘性或反粘性均不显著。

本文虽然首次证实了我国上市公司不仅存在费用粘性与费用反粘性，并进一步探索管理者预期对于我国费用管理的影响，但是由于主客观原因的限制，本文的研究还存在着样本数据的时间跨度较小、物价水平变动影响以及不同上市公司和管理者之间的个性差异等局限性，使得研究结论或多或少存在着误差。

但是，不论从理论深度还是实证研究方法上来看，运用实证方法证实在管理者预期的影响下，我国上市公司不仅存在费用粘性而且存在费用反粘性仅仅是个开始，笔者认为，尚有待后续研究者的补充和完善。因此，基于本文的研究结论，对后续的相关研究，提出如下建议：

(1) 在理论方面，"管理者预期"表象背后存在着对管理者心理进行分析的庞大而复杂的行为经济学理论分析系统，本文仅仅运用最基本的理论进行初步判断。后续的相关研究可以借鉴其理论成果和研究方法，进一步丰富对于"管理者乐观预期"和"管理者悲观预期"的理论支撑。

(2) 在实证研究方面，"管理者预期"的替代变量是一个可以深究的话题，本文仅运用营业收入的增减进行方向上的预判。鉴于最近在行为金融研究领域"管理者乐观主义对金融市场"的研究颇有建树，其中对于"管理者乐观主义"进行了较为系统的量化处理，后续的相关研究可以借鉴其研究方法，选择更为精准的替代变量。

(3) 在研究对象方面，本文仅研究了最易受管理者操控的"销售费用＋管理费用"，按照费用粘性理论多年的研究发展路径，后续的相关研究可以拓展到"营业成本"等领域，按照本文的研究模式，继续探索我国成本管理中存在的粘性或反粘性现象，使研究更为广泛和深入。

参考文献

[1] 陈磊、宋乐、施丹，2012，企业的成本粘性被高估了吗?《中国会计评论》，第3期，第3—16页。

[2] 龚启辉、刘慧龙、申慧慧，2010，地区要素市场发育、国有控股与成本和费用粘性，《中国会计评论》，第4期，第431—446页。

[3] 万寿义、王红军，2011，费用粘性成因的理论分析，《湖南财政经济学院学报》，第8期，第83—86页。

[4] Anderson, M. ,Banker, R. and Janakiraman, S. ,2003,Are selling,general,and administrative costs' sticky? *The Accounting Review*,Vol. 41,pp. 47—63.

[5] Anderson,S. and Lanen,W. ,2007,Understanding cost management: What can we learn from the evidence on "sticky costs"? Working paper.

[6] Balakrishnan,R. and Gruca, T. , 2008, Cost stickiness and core competency: A note, *Contemporary Accounting Research* ,Vol. 25,pp. 993—1006.

[7] Banker, R. ,Byzalov, D. and Plehn-Dujowich, J. ,2011,Sticky cost behavior: Theory and evidence,Working paper.

[8] Banker,R. and Chen,L. ,2006,Predicting earnings using a model based on cost variability and cost stickiness,*The Accounting Review*,Vol. 81,pp. 285—307.

[9] Banker, R. , Ciftci, M. and Mashruwala, D. , 2011, Managerial optimism and cost behavior, Working paper.

[10] Banker,R. , Hwang, I. and Mishra, B. K. ,2002, Product costing and pricing under long-term-capacity commitment,*Journal of Management Accounting Research* , Vol. 14,pp. 79—98.

[11] Baumgarten, D. , Bonenkamp, U. and Homburg, C. , 2012, The information content of the SG&A ratio,*Journal of Management Accounting Research* ,Vol. 22,pp. 1—22.

[12] Calleja, K. ,Steliaros, M. and Thomas, D. , 2006,A note on cost stickiness: Some international companies,*Management Accounting Research* , Vol. 17,pp. 127—140.

[13] Chen,C. and Lu, H. ,2008,Managerial empire building, corporate governance, and the asymmetric behavior of selling, general and administrative costs, Working paper.

[14] Cooper, R. and Kaplan, R. , Cost and effect, 1998a, *Using Integrated Cost Systems to Drive Profitability and Performance*, Harvard Business School Press, Boston.

[15] Russell Davidson and James G. MacKinnon, 1981, Several tests for model specification in the presence of alternative hypotheses, *The Econometric Society*, Vol. 49, No. 3,pp. 781—793.

[16] Dierynek, B. and Renders, A. ,2009,Earnings management incentives and the asymmetric behavior of labor costs,Working paper.

[17] Johnson-Laird, P. N. , Legrenzi, Paolo,Girotto, Vittorio, Legrenzi, Maria Sonino and Caverni, Jean-Paul, 1999, Naive probability: A mental model theory of extensional reasoning, *Psychological Review*,Vol. 106, No. 1,pp. 62—88.

[18] Kama, I. and Weiss, D. , 2010,Do managers' deliberate decisions induce sticky costs? Working paper.

[19] Rabin,M. and Schrag,J. L. ,1999, First impressions matter: A model of confirmatory bias,*The Quarterly Journal of Economics*,Vol. 114, No. 1,pp. 37—82.

[20] Subramaniam, C. and Weidenmier, L. , 2003, Additional evidence on the sticky behavior of costs,Working paper.

A Study of Managerial Expectation Impact on Cost Stickiness: From Chinese Listed Company Empirical Data

MAN WANG
(*Dongbei University of Finance and Economics*)
GE CAO
(*Bank of China Liaoning Branch*)
SHUI LIU
(*Dongbei University of Finance and Economics*)

Abstract Using data for China's listed companies in stock markets of Shanghai and Shenzhen over the period 2008—2011, this paper results in four dimensions: (1) Costs are sticky when conditioned on a sales increase in the prior period, but costs are in fact anti-sticky when conditioned on a prior period sales decrease; (2) Conflicting signals will lessen managers' confidence in expectation whereas confirmatory signals will strengthen managerial expectations, which will influence the extent of cost stickiness and anti-stickiness.

Key words Managerial Expectations, Cost Stickiness, Cost Anti-Stickiness, Cost Behavior

书　评
——展现新作力作，分享心得感受

本杂志开设书评栏目，旨在为国内或国外出版的新书提供一个展现的舞台、为读者提供一个分享交流读书心得的机会。

在当今学术界，尽管学术成就的象征越来越集中于在各大杂志上发表的论文，学术专著仍然有其重要和不可替代的地位。专著使作者能够有足够的篇幅来完整、系统地论述或论证某一主题，而这若分散在不同的文章中可能就会支离破碎。正是由于其在理论构建和论证方面的完整性，经典书籍的引用率也丝毫不亚于论文。例如，迈克尔·波特(Michael Porter)出版于1985年的《竞争优势——营造并保持最佳表现》(*Competitive Advantage: Creating and Sustaining Superior Performance*)，其引用率就达到4万多次。

正因为书籍在学术研究中的重要地位，书评一直是国际优秀杂志的重要栏目，书评的作者也往往是相关领域的学术权威。为有助于我们的读者在浩瀚的书海中更快捷地找到相关书籍，为使倾注了作者心血和智慧的好书得到更多读者的关注，也为了使更多的读者能分享您的读书心得，我们诚邀您通过以下方式参与、支持本栏目的建设：

1. 推荐好书

若您读到有价值的、与本杂志主题相关的书籍，或您写作出版了类似书籍，请向书评编辑推荐。本栏目内容包括管理会计以及与其相关的主题，如管理控制系统、内部控制、战略与决策、公司治理，或者是更广泛的管理或学术研究方法等领域；类型并不仅仅限于理论、学术专著，我们也欢迎相关的政策解读、教材，或者实务案例和报告；所推荐书籍可以是中文或英文、国内或海外出版，出版年限可往前追溯十年。

2. 撰写评论

我们期望书评不仅仅提供书的概述，而且指出其在理论或实务方面的创新和贡献，字数以1 000—2 000字为佳。

我们期待您的支持和参与。具体请与书评编辑李苹莉联系：p. li@mdx.ac.uk。

图书在版编目（CIP）数据

管理会计学刊.第5卷.第1期/汤谷良,肖泽忠主编.—北京:北京大学出版社,2014.6

ISBN 978-7-301-24146-2

Ⅰ.①管… Ⅱ.①汤… ②肖… Ⅲ.①管理会计-丛刊 Ⅳ.①F234.3-55

中国版本图书馆CIP数据核字(2014)第074737号

书　　名：管理会计学刊(第5卷第1期)
著作责任者：汤谷良　肖泽忠　主编
责 任 编 辑：李　娟　韩慧博
标 准 书 号：ISBN 978-7-301-24146-2/F·3934
出 版 发 行：北京大学出版社
地　　址：北京市海淀区成府路205号　100871
网　　址：http://www.pup.cn
电 子 信 箱：em@pup.cn　　QQ:552063295
新 浪 微 博：@北京大学出版社　@北京大学出版社经管图书
电　　话：邮购部62752015　发行部62750672　编辑部62752926
　　　　　出版部62754962
印　刷　者：北京大学印刷厂
经　销　者：新华书店
　　　　　787毫米×1092毫米　16开本　9.75印张　160千字
　　　　　2014年6月第1版　2014年6月第1次印刷
定　　价：30.00元
International Price: $30.00

《管理会计学刊》征订

《管理会计学刊》是中国境内首家专注管理会计研究的学术期刊，由对外经济贸易大学、北京大学、清华大学、中国人民大学、复旦大学、中山大学等22所高校组成的《管理会计学刊》理事会联合发起成立，北京大学出版社出版，主要面向国内高校会计教育界和学术界发行。

本刊集合国内外管理会计学术专家组成管理和编辑团队，定位于搭建中国管理会计与控制领域的权威发布平台。学刊内容涵盖：管理会计理论、管理控制系统、绩效评价与薪酬激励、成本管理与作业管理、供应链管理和跨组织管理会计、信息技术在管理会计与控制的应用、公司治理与组织控制等。

《管理会计学刊》为大16开，每期150页左右。本刊印刷装帧考究，内容深刻，极富学术参考价值和保存价值，是高等学校财务、会计专业教师和学生的重要参考。

我们诚邀海内外学者踊跃投稿和订阅，共同促进管理会计的学术繁荣与创新。

订阅地址：北京大学871-150信箱　　邮编：100871
联系电话：010-62752015　　传真：010-62753573　　联系人：邢丽华
电子邮箱：bdsd@pku.edu.cn　　网址：www.pup.cn

户名：北京大学出版社
开户行：工商银行北京海淀西区支行
账号：0200004509066138007
税号：110108H52628530

《管理会计学刊》征订单

（可复制）

每期定价：人民币**30元**			邮购价：人民币**40元**（含邮资）		
订户名称				联系人	
详细地址				邮　编	
电子邮箱		传真		电　话	
订阅期数	总第____期			份　数	每期　份
合计金额	人民币（大写）		￥　　元	汇款日期	
注：订刊款汇出后请立即将此订单邮寄、传真或E-mail到北京大学出版社北大书店，作为发行凭证，以便订户及时收到本刊。					

说明：1. 请到邮局汇款订阅。可随时订阅，一年起订。
2. 汇款时请务必将汇款人单位（地址）、姓名写清楚，以免影响邮寄。
3. 请勿电汇购书款，请勿在信中夹寄钱物。

JOURNAL OF MANAGEMENT ACCOUNTING STUDIES (JMAS)

Journal of Management Accounting Studies (JMAS) is the first academic journal dedicated to management accounting research in China. It is published by the Peking University Press and launched by the JMAS Council which is formed by 22 universities including University of International Business and Economics, Peking University, Tsinghua University, Renmin University, Fudan University and Sun Yat-sen University.

The management and editorial team of this journal consists of eminent management accounting scholars within and outside China. The aim of the journal is to provide a publication forum for research in management accounting and control. The areas where papers can be published include management accounting theory, management and control systems, performance evaluation and incentive pay, cost and operations management, supply chain management and inter-organizational management accounting, information technology and management accounting, and corporate governance.

Each issue of JMAS contains about 150 pages and is printed elegantly with quality paper. The table of contents and abstracts are also provided in English. The journal provides deep insights into the latest developments of management accounting research and makes an important reference for accounting and finance researchers, practitioners and students.

We warmly welcome submissions of papers and subscriptions from academics around the world.

JOURNAL OF MANAGEMENT ACCOUNTING STUDIES (JMAS)

Order Form

☐Institutions & Individuals US $30.00/Volume

Please enclose a check payable to *Journal of Management Accounting Studies* with this order form.

Subscription to	
☐ Vol. 1	☐ Vol. 5
☐ Vol. 2	☐ Vol. 6
☐ Vol. 3	☐ Vol. 7
☐ Vol. 4	☐ Vol. 8

Only checks are accepted

Currency Options	
☐ RMB	☐ Hong Kong dollar
☐ Euro	☐ US dollar

Name ____________________

Address ____________________

City/state/Zip/Country ____________________

Phone ( ) ____________ Fax ( ) ____________

E-mail ____________________

Please mail your order and check to *Journal of Management Accounting Studies*, UIBE Business School, Beijing 100029, China.